D1143013

BOTHAM'S BEDSIDE CRICKET BOOK

Ian Botham was born in 1955 and made his first-class debut for Somerset in 1974. When he was twenty-one he took five Australian wickets in his first day of Test innings (at Lord's). He holds the record for having scored 1000 runs and taken 100 wickets in the fewest Tests; he has scored 1000 runs in a single season. In 1981 his stupendous innings in Tests against the Australians (becoming the first man in England-Australia Tests to strike six sixes in an innings) and his lethal bowling saved the series and the Ashes for England. He is also the author of *Botham Down Under* (1983).

Kenneth Gregory was born in 1921. He is a writer by profession and has contributed to *The Times*, the *Guardian*, the *Spectator* and the *Illustrated London News*. He is the author of *The First Cuckoo* (1976), and *In Celebration of Cricket* (1978) and has contributed to *Barclays' World of Cricket* (1980). He is also the author, with Ray Illingworth, of *The Ashes: a Centenary* (1982).

BOTHAM'S BEDSIDE CRICKET BOOK

Ian Botham
and Kenneth Gregory

with drawings by Haro

FONTANA/Collins

First published by William Collins Sons & Co. Ltd 1982
First issued in Fontana Paperbacks 1983

Made and printed in Great Britain by
William Collins Sons & Co. Ltd, Glasgow

Originally published in hardback as
Botham's Choice.

Contents

Foreword

In the introduction to this book I say that good cricket is entertainment. Well, we've tried to entertain by reminding the reader that cricket – *worthwhile* cricket – is all a matter of great skill and fun.

In these pages you'll meet some of the Masters you would have loved to bat or bowl against – and some of the odd happenings behind the scenes. You'll meet some of the most extraordinary characters from the history of cricket and read of amazing events, some of which could simply never happen again.

We've enjoyed researching the material for the book and hope you'll enjoy reading the final selection – my choice. Except, of course, the last chapter. You must excuse my blushes over that Afterword – blame instead my co-author, Kenneth Gregory!

By Way of an Introduction

GREGORY: You don't know how fortunate you and your contemporaries are. When you do something outstanding in a Test match, every ball is televised; you're captured for all time. In fifty or a hundred years from now, people will know exactly what your two hundreds against Australia in 1981 were like in every detail.

BOTHAM: You mean that Hobbs, Bradman and Hammond rely on what was written about them? True. I agree, we are lucky. But it cuts both ways – your blobs are televised too.

GREGORY: So it's important that you're honest. If you talk as though the most you've done is score a scratchy half-century against a weak Minor County attack . . .

BOTHAM: No one will read the book!

GREGORY: And if you give the impression that you're Keith Miller, Gary Sobers and Mike Procter rolled into one . . .

BOTHAM: I'm a big-headed –

GREGORY: Exactly! First, let's put you in perspective. You started playing for Somerset in 1974 – only eight years ago. In other words, you grew up in an age of first-class cricket *and* limited over cricket.

BOTHAM: Yes. The John Player Sunday League was in its sixth year when I began. I remember a lot of the older chaps grousing about it, saying how they hated going from three-day games to 40 overs a side. I've been lucky there. I just can't imagine what it's like *not* to play both kinds of cricket. Perhaps if I were ten years older, I should hate the constant change. I just don't know.

Of course, I've only played in the modern age of seam bowling. I've never faced a great spinner of the flighty sort because they just don't exist today. More important, they couldn't exist today in England because the pitches are so slow. I've only played first-class cricket since 1974, but even during that time the pitches have got slower and slower. Blame who you will, it's a fact. Our pitches are made for seam bowlers, something we've got to live with.

GREGORY: You can't imagine what it was like to play against, say, Grimmett?

BOTHAM: I can imagine it. But I've got no idea if what I'm imagining is right. For example Perth can be very fast. I believe Arthur Mailey spun his leg-breaks and googlies prodigiously and I think I can imagine playing against him at Perth. Less than perfect footwork, and you're a goner! But I would have loved to play against him.

GREGORY: Barry Richards once tackled Bishen Bedi on a turner at Northampton; they both said what a privilege it was to face one another.

BOTHAM: And where was Bedi brought up? In India. Any slow bowler brought up in England soon learns to bowl 'flat'. If he doesn't he'll be hit – *and safely*. When you know you have time to adjust to a bowler it makes all the difference. Bring back faster wickets and gradually you'll produce flighty spinners. As it is, we have fine seam bowlers and ordinary seam bowlers. Occasionally, you produce a genuinely fast bowler, but even he finds our wickets against him. You've got to live with it.

I'm certain of one thing. You're always hearing people say how dull it is to watch four West Indian fast bowlers in one side. I know if England had four such bowlers, they'd play all of them!

GREGORY: Play to your own strength?

BOTHAM: Yes.

GREGORY: Who would you like in your side? Of fast bowlers, I mean?

BOTHAM: Michael Holding. I can't imagine a more perfect, or faster bowler. He's a great athlete. His run-up is a joy, though I admit a greater joy if you're watching him from the square-leg boundary. He's straight and does enough with the ball, though at his speed that doesn't really matter. I just don't believe there's ever been a greater *fast* bowler.

GREGORY: Who else do you prefer watching from deep square leg?

BOTHAM: Joel Garner! Six foot nine inches. Bowling from the Nursery End at Lord's, his hand is above the sightscreen! Speed is one thing, Joel's bounce is another. Well, how are you meant to play a good length ball which passes you – and he's very straight – at least waist high? If only Tony Greig hadn't stopped growing at six foot seven inches, or whatever it is, he may have had an answer. Put in a negative sense, Joel must be the finest defensive bowler in history. He also takes wickets. And plays for Somerset! Something I approve of.

GREGORY: Any other bowlers?

BOTHAM: The greatest bowler, technically, I've ever played against – probably ever will play against. A fast or fast-medium bowler must have a run-up which is precisely right for him to realize his maximum speed with the minimum effort to himself. He must be able to do exactly what he wants with the ball: swing it, cut it off the seam, pitch it where he wants to, know how to play on a batsman's weakness. He must be a supreme craftsman. If he is, he won't rely on inspiration, he'll do everything intentionally. Want to hear anything more about Dennis Lillee?

GREGORY: Yes! At Old Trafford in 1981, you twice hooked Lillee for 6. From the new ball!

BOTHAM: I'd been in for 20 minutes, so why not? The balls were making straight for my head and I didn't feel like ducking.

GREGORY: Good a reason as any other. Reminds me of a Neville Cardus story about Charlie Macartney – how he got a brute of a ball from Maurice Tate, got up on his toes and crashed it through the covers. When Cardus congratulated him on the stroke, Macartney said, 'When I saw the ball I felt "Cripes! One of us is for it." So it had to be Maurice.'

BOTHAM: What batting's all about. And we're meant to entertain the public. If you get a challenge, you react. You react according to what you are. If you know you can play a certain stroke, then why not play it?

GREGORY: Annoy the bowler?

BOTHAM: Of course. Batsmen often annoy me when I'm bowling.

GREGORY: Who annoys you most of all?

BOTHAM: You mean who makes me feel I'd be better off shooting rabbits? Two sorts of batsmen: those who make me wonder where to pitch the ball, and those who make me feel I shall still be bowling at them in a month's time. To me the greatest batsman in the world is Viv Richards. He can make you feel a fool; he's capable of playing a Test innings so that you wonder if you're taking part in a limited overs game. I'm quite sure that when Viv has an out-of-sorts look about him, it's because he's stale. Been overplaying.

GREGORY: No weak spots?

BOTHAM: He may have, I haven't noticed them! If he wants to, he can force balls outside the off-stump to mid-wicket, he can step back and hit leg-stump balls past cover. Then you bowl him the best ball you're capable of, and he defends with time to spare. Just as though he's saying 'Thank you!'

GREGORY: Who else makes you feel more like shooting rabbits?

BOTHAM: Clive Lloyd. His bat weighs a ton, and he hits the ball harder than anyone I know. He can reach anything and he likes short stuff. I once bowled him a bouncer when I was young – *younger*! and didn't know any better. I thought it was going through the Edgbaston scoreboard. Much safer to attack his off-stump because then he hits you on the ground. Not such a blow to dignity.

GREGORY: And non-West Indies?

BOTHAM: For my money Sunil Gavaskar is a very great batsman. West Indians, even the finest, don't like being contained. Gavaskar doesn't mind. He knows he'll most likely be batting at close of play. Wonderful judgement to any ball, sort of computer in his brain. The 221 he made against England at the Oval in 1979 was a masterpiece.

GREGORY: Len Hutton compared it to two great innings played during his first season for England in 1938 – McCabe at Trent Bridge and Hammond at Lord's.

BOTHAM: There's more than one way of making a bowler feel useless. You see, when you're bowling at Viv Richards, you keep telling yourself that anyone as brilliant will sooner or later get himself out. But with Gavaskar, he plays well within himself. Just goes on and on. His concentration never cracks, his technique is flawless. And he can score faster than he gives the impression of doing. He can place the ball exactly where he likes.

GREGORY: I once read of a Bradman innings – the fifth Test at Melbourne in 1936–7 – when he reached his hundred in 125 minutes with only 7 boundaries. Allen, Voce, Farnes, Hammond and Verity bowling – not a bad lot.

BOTHAM: A hell of a job to place a field to! You were bound to have close fielders in case he mis-cued – and you would have wanted three or four out deep.

GREGORY: Give the captaincy to Mike Brearley.

BOTHAM: Who else? He was a genius. He knew instinctively what you were thinking. He'd come up to you, look you in the eye – and read your brain.

GREGORY: A sympathetic captain?

BOTHAM: Yes. When necessary he could be strict. He'd tell you to try this or that – suggest some slight alteration in the field, tell you why he wanted it. If you were bowling below your best, he'd have you off – unless he knew that a certain batsman didn't like you. If you were out of luck, he'd whip you off at one end; 10 minutes later he'd have you on at the other. The best remark about Mike came from Rodney Hogg after that tour of Australia when Rodney took 41 wickets in the series. 'The difference between the two sides is Brearley. He's got a degree in *people*.' Mike would read a game as though he'd been playing for a hundred years. He was uncanny.

And it was fun playing under him because he made you play at your best. When you play at your best, you're happy. It was fun in that sense.

GREGORY: Can you really play cricket when it's not played in your way?

BOTHAM: So long as there's a challenge, yes. I'd loved to have seen a great batsman playing on an old-fashioned sticky wicket, or a great spinner throwing the ball up and making the batsmen use their feet. Challenge is everything. When you hit Dennis Lillee for 4 you think, 'That was good!' When you hit a bad bowler, you don't react in the same way. No tension. No tension, no challenge. Dull cricket. It all comes down to entertainment.

1

The Champion

Andrew Lang (1844–1912) was a Scots poet and lover of cricket. He argued the game had started BC when the batsman defended with a club a hole in the ground into which his opponent tried to pitch the ball. The champion in those days was an Irish demi-god, Cuchulainn, who took on everyone in sight. His greatest success was against 150 Colts of Ulster, when an abbreviated scoresheet ran as follows:

150 COLTS OF ULSTER, bowled Cuchulainn 0

BOWLING		Overs	Maidens	Runs	Wickets
Cuchulainn		37.2	37	0	150
CUCHULAINN	not out				1

It will be observed that the 4-ball over was then in vogue.

2

The Strange Fate of J. Marshall

Unusual dismissals sometimes occur in the best circles.

England v South Africa at the Oval, 1951
L. Hutton, obstructing the field 27

South Africa v England at Cape Town, 1956–7
W. R. Endean, handled ball 3

Both batsmen doubtless felt somewhat aggrieved by what had happened, though they had less cause to than a certain Pakistani cricketer who – in the final of the Quaid-I-Azam Trophy at Karachi in 1958–9 – went down in the score-book thus:

Abdul Aziz, did not bat, dead 0

Which brings us to the strange fate of a Yorkshireman, immortalized in the *Sheffield Iris* of 2 August 1842:

J. Marshall, burnt ball 0

Oddly, this dismissal did not provoke comment in the newspaper's leader columns: perhaps oddities were taken for granted in the Sheffield of 1842. All we know is that, like Hutton, J. Marshall was an opening batsman and that the captain of the opposing side was A. Dunnett. Dunnett was the game's top scorer – he made 7.

It's all very well to say that Marshall hit one delivery into a bonfire, that the fieldsman appealed and an umpire gave the batsman out. Under any Laws, that decision would be unlikely.

The only possible explanation of Marshall's fate is a simple one. It's justified by the fact that Marshall was an opening bat and took first ball of an innings. The night before the game, Dunnett applied himself to Marshall's bat (Marshall's club possessed two bats), roughening it with a file. Next, he coated the ball with phosphorus.

On the morrow Dunnett bowled the first over to Marshall who struck the initial delivery high into the heavens. An appeal found the umpire, a staunch chapel man, swearing he would sign the pledge – and giving Marshall out.

Any more likely explanation will be gratefully received by the publishers – but not paid for.

3

Martha's Son

In May 1866 a youth of seventeen played for the Gentlemen of England against Oxford University. To his dismay he got himself caught at short-leg, going neither forward nor back but merely half-cock. Very soon some terrible words were heard from inside a tent: 'Willie, haven't I told you over and over again how to play that ball?' The reply was a muttered, 'Yes, mama.' After more words of criticism, the youth was told to go out and practise the shot. Mrs Martha Grace had spoken; William Gilbert Grace obeyed.

Queen Victoria was on the throne, Mrs Grace ruled at Downend near Bristol. Her husband, Dr Henry Mills Grace, had included his fourth son in the West Gloucestershire eleven when the boy was nine; not very successfully, for during the years 1857–9 young William Gilbert achieved these figures – Innings 19, Times not out 4, Runs 20, Highest score 5, Average 1.33. But Mrs Grace was not disturbed. In 1860 she wrote to George Parr, who ran the England XI, recommending the inclusion of her son, E. M. Grace – adding that his brother would one day be a far superior player as his back stroke was well-founded.

Martha Grace recognized talent when she saw it; more, she had bowled at William Gilbert in the orchard at home. In later years she would sit in the enclosure at Clifton and receive famous cricketers. Unfortunately she disapproved of left-handed batsmen as a matter of principle, and on them she cast a beady eye. Left-handers therefore avoided the presence. When she died in 1884 Gloucestershire were playing Lancashire at Old Trafford. Flags were lowered, the game abandoned, and W. G. and E. M. hurried home. Today the

Births and Deaths columns of *Wisden* include the name of only one woman – Mrs H. M. Grace.

A great cricketer can be judged only in the context of his age. Jack Hobbs towards the end of his life watched play at the Oval; the negative bowling impressed him – 'I don't see how I could have scored against this.' A pause for reflection: 'Of course, it would never have got me out!' Bradman would today receive far fewer balls per hour than he did in the Thirties, and so score more slowly. All we can say of W. G. Grace is that he dominated cricket in his time, and was also sufficiently a master when playing from memory that he could dominate bowlers of the next generation. In 1902 – in his fifty-fourth year – he faced the bowling of S. F. Barnes in the Gentlemen *v* Players match and made 82. Four years later against the professionals' attack he made 74.

A less elegant great batsman than Grace never lived. Endowed with a tremendous physique, he relied on perfect timing and placing: the effect was one of an awesome power, relentlessly applied. During his prime, the wickets he played on were often appalling: fast bowlers aimed where they would and Grace tamed them. The Gentlemen *v* Players match at Lord's in 1868 persuaded one observer that *he* would have worn a fencing mask, a Life Guardsman's cuirass and a tin stomach-warmer. The best professionals of England totalled 111 and 113 from the bat (Grace 10 wickets for 81), ten amateurs in their first innings scraping 59, and W. G. 134 not out.

In 1885 at Scarborough the Gentlemen won by an innings, though the Players included William Barnes, Attewell, Flowers and Ulyett, who had recently bowled England to victory in Australia, and the left-hander Peate. Ten Gentlemen managed 83, Grace 174. Small wonder Tom Emmett said Grace should be made to play with a 'littler bat', and that on cricket grounds the sign went up

ADMISSION SIXPENCE
If Dr Grace plays one shilling

After all, Grace was a most eminent Victorian who had superb entertainment value. How he managed to pass his medical exams remains something of a mystery: 'Reading ruins the eyes for batting.' There was always a small boy trying, generally with success, to burst out of W. G. Once, after dinner, he intrigued his hostess 'by marching round the drawing-room bearing the coal scuttle on his head for a helmet, with the poker carried as a sword'. Doubtless hoping his friend Frederick Spofforth would appear pretending to be Saladin. Larger – and somewhat more absurd – than life were the Victorians.

How good *was* Grace? In his day, incomparable: during the years 1867–76 he played 280 completed innings with an average of 57, the next best figure of 36 being obtained by combining the ten most productive seasons of *seven* other men. (He also took 840 wickets.) Then how good was he compared with later master batsmen? In 1867–76 against the Players, often on impossible pitches, he played 41 innings, average 65. During the ten years 1919–28 against the Gentlemen, generally on the best pitches devised by man, Jack Hobbs played 34 innings, average 71.

Inevitably, the name of Bradman comes to mind. But not even he could overwhelm his contemporaries as Grace did his. We do not seek to compare three cricketers of genius, merely to show them in the context of their respective ages. Twice – between March 1929 and February 1932 and January 1936 and January 1948 – Bradman made 11 Test centuries in 20, or 22, innings. Grace and Hobbs also made 11 centuries during their great periods for the Gentlemen or Players.

But Hobbs and Bradman were not alone in their splendour, other members of their sides or of the opposition also scoring heavily.

1936–48	Bradman	11 centuries, other batsmen	31
1929–32	Bradman	11 centuries, other batsmen	18
1919–28	Hobbs	11 centuries, other batsmen	27
1867–76	Grace	11 centuries, other batsmen	4

Grace was in the habit of bowling the other side out!

One thing he did have in common with Bradman – an absence of pity on bowlers after establishing himself. Bradman's 117 century innings in first-class cricket averaged 216, Grace's 126 century innings 182. Of the Titan's Indian summer in 1895 – 1,000 runs in May and in his forty-seventh year – one occasion only shall be singled out. At Lord's for the Gentlemen, W. G. had to perform on a very fast and fiery wicket against Tom Richardson and Arthur Mold. A few months previously Richardson had dismissed thirty-two

Australians (twenty-six bowled) to win the Ashes for England; Mold was the fastest *persistent* chucker of all time. At Lord's in 1895 Grace made 118.

Grace created modern batting. His attack was based on a superb defence; he once stopped four successive shooters at Lord's and the ground rose to him: four shooters which Grace knew full well might have risen to strike either fingers or chest! J. C. Shaw, a length bowler if ever there was one, summed up W. G. well: 'It ain't a bit of use my bowling good 'uns to him now; it's a case of I can bowl where I likes and he can hit where he likes.' Ranjitsinhji declared that he himself had only begun as a bat where Grace had left off.

Did W. G. sometimes appear to bend the rules? Of course! Did he ever cheat? The classic answer came from the old Gloucestershire bowler, Fred Roberts: ''E were too clever for that!' We must remember that when the Doctor played, admission was one shilling. Let Lord Harris have the last word: 'He was always a most genial, even-tempered, considerate companion, and of all the many cricketers I have known the *kindest* as well as the best.'

4

Hints for Touring Captains

On his first Canadian tour in 1872, W. G. Grace made a classic after-dinner speech.

'Mr Chairman, I beg to thank you for the honour you have done me. I never saw better bowling than I have seen today, and I hope to see as good wherever I go.'

With that, W. G. sat down. On five later occasions, he made *almost* the same speech – deleting the word 'bowling' and substituting 'ground', 'batting', 'fellows', 'pretty ladies' and (for even he could be eloquent) 'oysters'.

5

Bunkered

Samuel Moses James Woods was born in Sydney, brought to England when fourteen and eventually played for Cambridge in four matches against Oxford: he took 36 wickets at small cost. Odd things happened to Sam. In 1888 he was called upon by the touring Australians and appeared in the three Tests; seven years later he tackled W. G. Grace on the occasion of the great man's hundredth century: 'I bowled him a shooter when he was in the 90s, and he didn't stop it; he hit it for 4 to square-leg.' The following winter he went to South Africa with an England side when George Lohmann took 35 Test wickets at 5.85 each. (Against Australia Lohmann was less successful: 77 wickets at 12.98.)

Not surprisingly, Sammy Woods played for Somerset. In later years, after retirement, he sought self-expression of a kind in golf. W. A. Darlington, drama critic of the *Daily Telegraph*, once enjoyed Sam's company in a foursome of fewer than 18 holes. Two respectable drives pleased both couples, and conversation touched on the perfection of the universe. Suddenly Sam strode off, slammed his ball a vast distance, then stepped into a bunker. Parting the sand, he reached down and pulled out a bottle.

The bottle was full; some minutes later it was not. Surprisingly, the first hole was halved in 5. The second hole saw the same procedure, one pair winning in 9. The round was abandoned after the eighth, when both pairs achieved a dozen putts, insisting (a) the hole had shrunk, then (b) disappeared.

6

God Bless

Lord Justice Norman Birkett must rank as one of the finest after-dinner speakers of all time; certainly on cricket he was incomparable. He had also brought himself up well; as a boy he said his prayers every night, asking the Almighty to take care of the Surrey side. Naming them one by one, Birkett ended, 'And God bless leg-byes.' Naturally such prayers had due effect, Surrey winning the County Championship nine times between 1887 and 1899. Non-Surrey men will claim that a team with George Lohmann, Tom Richardson and W. H. Lockwood to bowl, and with Bobby Abel to head the batting, would have needed Divine intervention to prevent them from winning.

It's that 'And God bless leg-byes' that still rankles. There was a time when batsmen were permitted to use their pads and urge the ball to third man or long-leg – all runs accruing were entered in scorebooks under Extras or Sundries, with details frequently omitted. The great Herbert Strudwick once said, 'Never think about byes. Keep your mind on getting the batsman out. The man you let off will soon up more runs than any byes you miss.' All very well, but hardly likely to massage a wicketkeeper's ego.

Small boys obliged to stand behind the stumps in public parks wisely held a jacket which they dropped on fast deliveries. The Cambridge University keeper against MCC in 1842 clearly had not heard of this wheeze – or he preferred to keep within the rules of the game. Of MCC's 197, some 66 came from assorted extras, 49 of them byes. Three years previously in the University game at Lord's, the Oxford keeper conceded only 24 byes, but Extras reached 70 on account of 46 wides.

Good wicketkeepers have nightmare days. 'Tich' Cornford of Sussex stood up to Maurice Tate and ended his career with over one thousand dismissals. But when MCC toured Australia and New Zealand in 1929–30, Cornford set some sort of record. In successive completed innings, New Zealand made 440 (Extras 43, 17 of them byes) and 387 (Extras 57, 31 of them byes).

In the mid-fifties the wicket at Northampton was, to put it mildly, doctored for the left-arm googly spin of George Tribe. Frank Tyson heaved manfully on the beast but generally to small avail. Once he bowled an intended bouncer to Peter May who went back, waited – and played the ball down from knee-high. But Tribe was awful to face. Imagine then a *reserve* wicketkeeper compelled to take a spinner far more difficult than George Tribe. At Northampton in 1955 Godfrey Evans was absent from the Kent side, his understudy one A. W. Catt. His tormentor was Douglas Wright, a *medium-pace* bowler of leg-breaks and googlies which leapt from the pitch. *Wisden* states that Catt's movements were impeded by sunburn:

Northants 374 (Extras 73, 48 of them byes – and Norman Birkett's 'God bless leg-byes' 23).

An out-of-form wicketkeeper must simply hope he will have Dr Grace at the crease. When the Titan made 288 against Somerset in his golden summer of 1895, the Rev. A. P. Wickham who was keeping wicket said that only three deliveries passed the old man's bat: these the Champion could not reach.

7

Negative Tactics

Reluctant as we are to drag in the past and so give rise to an international incident capable of splitting the world of cricket, we feel bound to draw the reader's attention to a most regrettable occasion when the fielding side did all in its power to shatter a batsman's concentration. To emphasize the enormity of the offence, we would translate the events from past to present and ask if, say, Chris Tavaré might not justly complain to MCC, TCCB, the House of Commons *and* the United Nations if subjected to these time-wasting, concentration-disturbing and unsporting reactions.

Between each delivery from Holding, Roberts, Garner and Croft, Tavaré is subjected to (a) indecent noise from the fielders, (b) a display of gymnastics from the fielders, and (c) patting on the back. We do not suggest how he would feel; we merely ask the reader to feel for himself. Was it cricket?

In 1900 a West Indies touring side visited England. It was captained by R. S. A. Warner (brother of P. F.), and included Learie Constantine's father, Lebrun. On 28 June the West Indians began a match against Gloucestershire at Bristol. During the afternoon Gilbert Jessop batted for an hour – not more, not less, just 60 minutes. In this time he scored 157. He had been at the crease for a matter of 10 minutes when he struck a ball out of the ground in the general direction of the Bristol Channel. The West Indians laughed.

But when Jessop repeated the stroke – and the authorities hired a cab driver to follow, gather and return the ball, one West Indian showed his feelings by doing a cartwheel. This, surely, constituted an assault on the batsman's concentration. Worse was to come; before long the West Indians greeted each

Jessop stroke by falling to the ground where they lay shrieking with laughter and kicking their heels in the air.

We may safely assume that today the TCCB would censure the West Indians for time-wasting. There was the umpire with a cricket ball in his hand (not the last cricket ball to be hit out of the ground but some tattered object, its shine removed by rolling down a hill) and the bowler was on his back. True, Jessop didn't appear to be put out by this behaviour, but it did somewhat retard his rate of scoring. All we are agreed upon is that if the West Indians had kept on their feet and played properly, Jessop must have made many more during his hour at the crease.

A few weeks later Gloucestershire travelled north to Bradford. A match with the county champions, Yorkshire, was a very different matter from one with temperamental West Indians. With George Hirst, Schofield Haigh and Wilfred Rhodes to contend with, a batsman must think. There may have been county attacks as good as Yorkshire's of 1900, there have been none better. Besides, Rhodes had worked out a way of containing Jessop: 'All you have to do,' he said to Hirst, 'is bowl a foot outside off-stump.'

Noting that in 1900 a batsman scored 6 only if he hit a ball *out of the ground*, and that a stroke landing on the roof of the football stand counted only 4 at Bradford, we shall commend the sporting behaviour of the champions. In his first innings Jessop made 104 in 70 minutes, with a 6 over the football stand off Rhodes. But when Gloucestershire were set a target of 328 to win, Jessop scored 139 in 95 minutes. Rhodes employed his new tactics to keep Jessop quiet and was seven times hit right over the top of the football stand. The crowd roared their approval, George Hirst grinned and Rhodes clucked.

But not once did the Yorkshire side perform cartwheels, not once did they fall to the ground, shrieking with laughter and kicking their heels in the air. The moral is clear: take your cricket seriously.

8

Prayers Unanswered

Albert Knight of Leicestershire was a very good batsman. He was also a deeply religious man. Having taken guard at the start of an innings, he would bow his head in prayer while the bowler waited.

'For the runs I am about to score, I thank Thee, O Lord.'

Walter Brearley of Lancashire, a rumbustious fast bowler, was appalled by Knight seeking to enlist the Almighty's aid, and said he would report him to the MCC.

At Melbourne in 1903–4 Plum Warner included Knight in the England team. Inevitably there was attempted liaison with Him on High. First A. J. Hopkins hit Len Braund in the general direction of Knight, who brought off a fine catch. As the batsman walked away, Knight sank to his knees and gave thanks.

Alas, two Australian bowlers, Tibby Cotter and Hugh Trumble, decided that pace and off-spin are more potent than prayer:

Knight	b	Cotter			0
Knight	c	Kelly	b	Trumble	0

9

Summer of Deception

The South Africans who toured England in 1907 were unfortunate; so, too, were most of the Englishmen who tried to bat against them. The South Africans were accustomed to playing on the mat, English batsmen to bowling of moral pretensions; the South Africans had been warned that an English summer – May to August – would give about eight inches of rain, only to strike a year when May and June alone contributed twenty-two inches. It was all very vexing; in due course *Wisden* wrote sagely of 'the new development'.

What was 'the new development'? Well, first let it be understood that any bowler who went through a full English season (in the days when there were full English seasons, that is before the arrival of much one-day cricket) and took a wicket every 6 overs was a capable performer: he was indeed an attacking bowler. Trueman and Statham at their peak would take a wicket every 36 balls; so would Lock; Larwood was even more rapid in his means of destruction. And in 1907?

At the end of 26 first-class matches, the South African bowling averages intrigued. Eight of every 10 wickets had been captured by one of four bowlers – not in itself an unusual occurrence, but phenomenal in terms of average and balls per wicket. Six English county bowlers averaged between 32 and 36 balls per wicket. Now consider the South African four:

	Wkts.	Av.	Balls/wkt.
R. O. Schwarz	137	11.79	31
G. C. White	56	14.73	30
A. E. Vogler	119	15.62	30
G. A. Faulkner	64	15.82	36

All were 'googly' bowlers, though they themselves preferred the term 'wrong 'un'. Their captain, Percy Sherwell, had no doubt of his tactics – in all but three of the first-class games he played at least three of his deceivers, in fourteen he played the lot. Should one man, even two men, be out of form, it didn't matter – a whole summer devoted, as we might surmise, to leg-breaks and googlies. So surmising, we should be wrong. One of the South African quartet did not bowl leg-breaks.

Reginald Schwarz was an Englishman, an international half-back at rugby football. At Cambridge he presented himself as a batsman but failed to gain his Blue. After playing for Middlesex, he left for South Africa in 1902, returning to England a couple of years later with a touring side presumably short of batsmen. Meanwhile Schwarz had given thought to B. J. T. Bosanquet's fairly recent invention, the off-break bowled with what seemed a leg-break action. (The recipients of Bosanquet's odd delivery deemed it 'unfair'; the bowler disagreed – 'Not unfair, merely immoral.') Suddenly, Schwarz saw how it was done.

By 1907 he was a master of the newly discovered ball. BUT he had also reached a certain conclusion – namely that a wrist spinner without command of pitch was useless. Schwarz therefore abandoned the leg-break and bowled nothing but googlies. Here there was only one difficulty to be overcome, the amount of spin to be used. On a good wicket, Schwarz broke anything from six to eighteen inches, but on a sticky he brought the ball back a yard. Very slow through the air, Schwarz came off the pitch at incredible pace. With six men on the on-side, he could of course be played as an ordinary off-spinner. However . . .

Schwarz was merely one of four googly bowlers. Faulkner and White could be played as the English leg-spinners Len Braund and Joe Vine were with flowing strokes through the covers *except that they bowled the googly.* Vogler was an altogether different matter. Having for some overs swung the ball, he then reverted to the new method, coming in off a twelve-yard run and delivering the ball off a fast-bowler's leap at *medium pace*. The England captain of 1907, R. E. Foster, had no hesitation in acclaiming Vogler as the finest bowler in the world – that is he placed him in front of Hirst and Rhodes, and of the Australians Trumble, Noble and Saunders. In retrospect, Foster should have perhaps have said 'the finest bowler in first-class cricket'. Playing for Staffordshire in the Minor Counties Championship was S. F. Barnes.

Schwarz could in theory be played as an ordinary off-spinner. However batting is often mind over matter. Here were four bowlers all promising leg-breaks, three whose stock deliveries were indeed leg-breaks. Two, Vogler and Faulkner, had googlies which came back like a knife; White relied more on the top-spinner for his 'relief' ball; Schwarz certainly promised but did not bowl leg-breaks. Small wonder that batsmen did not know what to expect, or believe they might expect.

The three Tests of 1907 were fascinating. At Lord's, when England won the toss (as she did on each occasion), Vogler bowled like a hero as the home side made 428 at 75 runs an hour. The pundits in the Long Room clucked – and, of course, with good reason. England had crawled! She had in a way. The first 5 wickets, and the last 4, realized 283 runs at about a run a minute. In the Golden Age this was appalling whatever the bowling. But between whiles there was a bright interlude when England's sixth wicket added 145 in 75 minutes. Given that Braund, who made 104 without ever feeling at ease (his own admission), was at one end, students will have no problem in identifying his partner. Gilbert Jessop made 93 before falling to a catch in front of the sightscreen. In the circumstances Vogler's 47.2–12–128–7 was memorable.

Here we must ask a question which will probably go unanswered: did members of the Pennsylvania University side touring England in 1907 attend the first day of the Lord's Test? They most certainly could have if, at close of play, they had caught a train from Paddington to Bristol where – the following day – they were to play Clifton College. Among the Pennsylvanians was an Australian studying dentistry; against Clifton he would have match figures of 12 for 85; some four years and more later, against the great England team of 1911–12, he would take 32 wickets in the series. H. V. ('Ranji') Hordern, first of the Australian googly masters.

Back to Lord's 1907. The second day was eccentric. Dave Nourse made 62 in South Africa's first innings, and Faulkner 44; nine other batsmen totalled 22. England's attack, consisting of George Hirst, Ted Arnold (5 for 37), Colin Blythe and Len Braund, was just too good. Following on 288 behind, the tourists seemed without hope. But Percy Sherwell disagreed; he went in first and made 115 in an hour and three-quarters.

The third day was rained out, leaving further discussion of the googly for Leeds where the wicket was a brute.

Sodden at the start, it grew progressively worse under persistent heavy showers. England won by 53 runs, the 4 completed innings producing only one individual score above 30 – C. B. Fry, a superb 54 in England's second attempt. Colin Blythe finished with 15 wickets for 99 runs, then collapsed from nervous strain. Leeds was the famous occasion when Faulkner started the game with 6 for 17, the googly men reminding one England batsman of having to play Johnny Briggs through the air and Tom Richardson off the pitch – translated into modern terms, Bishen Bedi through the air and Dennis Lillee off the pitch! An exaggeration of sorts but understandable.

An honourable draw at the Oval concluded the series, whereupon the pundits discussed 'the new development'. How effective would the googly have been in a dry summer? That question, alas, was never answered, but others were. In 1909–10 a good, but by no means fully representative, England side toured South Africa, losing the series by three games to two. Vogler took 36 wickets and Faulkner 29. BUT a young batsman named Hobbs averaged 67. How did he play googly bowling on the mat? No problem at all. When the ball is pitched up, you simply use your feet and kill the spin; when it's short, you go back, select your stroke – and hit it.

And the googly on perfect Australian pitches? In 1910–11 South Africa were given a dusty answer by Victor Trumper who averaged 94 in the series, employing the same simple methods of Hobbs (simple, that is, if you were Hobbs or Trumper). Schwarz alone succeeded – 25 wickets at 26 each; White did not tour, being replaced by Syd Pegler; Vogler did tour but was in poor health; while Faulkner was ineffective. However this great cricketer did play Test innings of 62, 43, 204, 8, 56, 115, 20, 80, 52 and 92 for a total of 732 runs. And there, from South Africa's point of view, the matter of the googly more or less ended – though Xenophon Balaskas did win the Lord's Test of 1935, and with it the series.

In South Africa during the thirties turf wickets superseded matting, a new race of finger spinners gradually taking over. Of the famous earlier quartet, only Vogler survived (Schwarz and White had both been killed in the Great War) to appreciate the rich irony of 1935–6 when Victor Richardson's Australians carried all before them. Their instruments of torture were a couple of over-the-wrist men, Grimmett and O'Reilly. Also in the Australian party was the left-arm googly bowler, Chuck Fleetwood-Smith.

1907 to 1935–6 was a long time in cricket terms. There was, however, a link. The same Dave Nourse who made 62 at Lord's in the former year appeared for Western Province in March 1936. As Tiger O'Reilly took 6 for 35, Nourse made a confident 55. The score book entered his name as A. D. Nourse, senior. He was fifty-eight.

10

The Stance

Myth has it that W. G. Grace spent much of his time being hit on the pads and – before the bowler's umpire could answer some lusty appeal – declaiming, 'I'm not out! And I'm not going!' On the other hand we should remember that W.G. often explained why, placing his feet as he did, he couldn't possibly be out leg-before-wicket. That is to say, he was not – like Arthur Shrewsbury – a supreme master of pad-play as a second line of defence.

Maybe, after all, the Doctor was right. He insisted that a batsman should not move the back foot; the fact that Grace did in photographs taken by George Beldham proves only that he did when illustrating someone else's technique. Anyway, few will disagree that Grace, Hobbs and Bradman were pretty effective batsmen.

They had one thing in common: throughout their first-class careers, each was bowled or leg-before-wicket once in every 2.8 innings. BUT, whereas Hobbs was leg-before-wicket once every 9.6 innings, and Bradman once every 10 innings, Grace succumbed in like fashion only once every 25 innings. W.G.'s method meant he was far more likely to be bowled.

Which suggests that W.G. may have had just a *little* right to react as he was said to have done when struck on the pads.

11

Music Hath Charms

George Gunn was troubled. Not by the Australian bowling but by what he was made to hear. George was batting at Sydney on 13 December 1907 and batting well. Jack Saunders and Gerry Hazlitt presented no problems, and neither did Armstrong, Noble and Macartney. Gunn roused Tibby Cotter by asking when was he going to bowl his fast one. Cotter's pace persuaded all batsmen save George Gunn that he was very fast.

Sammy Carter, the Australian wicketkeeper, was an undertaker and therefore the most courteous of men. Noting that Gunn frequently frowned he said, 'Anything wrong?' Gunn first flicked Cotter off his eyebrows and then replied, 'That band over there.' The band was playing light airs and dances. 'What about it?' queried Carter. 'The cornet,' replied Gunn, 'out of tune. Flat.'

That Gunn made a brilliant century, and 74 in the second innings, is neither here nor there. The New South Wales Cricket Association did not apologize to the batsman who showed his indifference by making another century in the final Test at Sydney.

If, of course, a band had been playing at Perth when Dennis Lillee tried out his aluminium bat, the complaint would have been the other way about.

'Why aren't you playing?' the conductor would have said to the first oboe.

'I refuse to, that chap's bat is out of tune.'

12

1911

The English summer of 1911 is best remembered because it preceded a tour of Australia when the MCC side was one of the greatest ever to visit that country. However, strange things happened in 1911. S. F. Barnes finished sixty-ninth in the first-class bowling averages; indeed, when the MCC Australian party appeared at the Scarborough Festival, Barnes was flogged – though Jessop's century came at only a run a minute.

On the other hand, Barnes did well for Staffordshire in the Minor Counties competition. Against the All Indian visitors his figures were 15.5–9–14–5 and 12.3–6–15–9. Unfortunately for the tourists, their finest batsman, Major K. M. Mistri, could appear in only three games – 'his duties keeping him in close attendance on the Maharajah of Patiala'. What His Highness was doing, *Wisden* did not make clear, but it was rumoured that the Maharajah would agree to bat only if afforded a fourteen-gun salute.

The unfairest criticism in 1911 was heaped upon C. B. Fry. It was all the fault of Jessop. The great hitter's 7 centuries were scored at 80 runs an hour. Against Hampshire at Southampton he made 153 and 123 not out. Doing his best for the home side, Fry made 258 not out. The press told him in no uncertain terms what they thought of him; the mildest comment came from *Wisden* – 'he exercised considerable caution'.

Fry's 258 not out was made at 50 runs an hour.

13

Horticulturally

Spectators looked at the scorecard and willed it to happen. It did – on Saturday, 12 July 1913, and probably on other occasions as well. The ground was Derby, the visitors Sussex; the home side's wicketkeeper was George Beet, its first-change bowler Fred Root (later of Worcestershire and England). In the Sussex second innings the scorers were able to inscribe:

H. P. Chaplin c Beet b Root 23

14

Salute to Alletson

Edwin Boaler Alletson's physique – he was over six foot tall and weighed fifteen and a half stone – was generally more impressive than his cricket. During nine seasons before the Great War, this Notts professional played 179 innings, average 18.59, and took 33 wickets at 19.02. But his physique enabled him to achieve one innings (his only century) so remarkable that he entered the record books. While over-rates remain at their present absurd figure, it is unlikely Alletson will ever be dislodged from his pinnacle.

Alletson's innings just happened. First, the background. On 18 May 1911 at Hove, Notts batted against Sussex and made a modest 238. Alletson, suffering from a sprained wrist, contributed 7. Sussex then found the visitors' bowling friendly and reached 414. Alletson was allowed 1 over from which 3 runs were scored. 176 in arrears, Notts reached 127 for 1 in their second innings before subsiding to 185 for 7. The time was now 12.40 on the third day; Notts were 9 runs ahead with only 3 wickets to fall.

Early that day Alletson had gone for a sea bathe in the hope it would do his injured wrist good. Carrying a 2 lb 3 oz bat, he joined George Lee in the middle. Between 12.40 and 1.22 or thereabouts, the two added 73 before Lee was bowled by Leach. 258 for 8. Oates, the Notts wicketkeeper, came in; having scored a single, he was bowled by the second ball of Leach's next over. The clock showed 1.30, so the players adjourned for lunch: Notts 260 for 9, Alletson 47 not out.

So far Alletson had played defensively – 47 in 50 minutes, with five 4s, two 3s, four 2s and thirteen 1s – the sort of innings which was an everyday occurrence in the Golden Age. After lunch he watched the Notts No. 11, Tom Riley, prepare to face Leach. Whether Leach bowled straight and was stopped, or bowled wide of the stumps and ignored, is not recorded. The 4 remaining balls of his unfinished over failed to dismiss Riley – the most fortunate failure in cricket history.

Alletson girded his loins, wriggled his injured wrist and decided to give a testimonial to the effects of a bathe in the sea. His captain, A. O. Jones, had told him to 'have a go'. Right! But to start with, he must keep the ball down. Nine off Killick, then 9 off Leach – 20 from 2 overs, Riley obliging with two singles. Alletson now thought it safe to follow through, so Killick's next over realized 22. The wielder of a 2 lb 3 oz bat was now seeing the ball.

Two deliveries short of a length outside the off-stump could not be driven. Alletson played back: one back stroke smashed the pavilion clock, the other broke a window and wrecked the bar. Sussex Members went to earth. Alletson also drove in an arc between long-on and extra-cover. Five 6s were struck over the South Stand, one over the building where the Sports Club now stands. Making no attempt to reach the pitch of the ball, Alletson just drove.

He was slowed down through losing five balls, the Sussex Club running out of replacements. From 7 overs bowled after lunch, Alletson received 37 deliveries and scored 115 runs – a rate of 310 per 100 balls. A bowling change reduced his act of mayhem to more decent proportions. Even so, when Alletson was caught off Cox on the straight drive boundary, he had made 189 in 90 minutes. Of his dismissal it may be said that the fielder, C. L. A. Smith, was leaning back and made the catch with one foot back and with his head against the stand – so 'breaking the boundary'.

In short, Alletson's last stroke should have been another 6! The batsman wasn't worried, for Notts now had a chance to win the match. But had this last stroke counted 6 – and had Alletson then made another 5 in, say, 5 minutes – then his 200 would have taken 95 minutes. The fastest double centuries ever scored – by Jessop and Clive Lloyd – were both timed at 120 minutes. Therein lies the absurdity of Alletson's innings.

But it was the post-lunch Alletson who bewilders us. In 40 minutes he made 142. Subtract the 2 minutes it must have taken Leach, with a long run, to bowl four balls to Riley – and the time wasted while balls were found to replace those hit out of the ground; 35 minutes seems a more likely duration for the

Alletson onslaught. Including the ball from which he was adjudged out, Alletson faced 51 deliveries here illustrated. One Killick over contained two no-balls: Riley's contributions are ringed.

Killick	Leach	Killick	Leach	Killick	Leach
0441 ⓪①①	24201	604246	⓪③ 4063	44021 ⓪	46043 ⓪
Killick	A. E. Relf	Cox	A. E. Relf	Cox	
46604446 ①	00004	⓪⓪⓪⓪⓪③	① 42261	440W	

The best way to salute Alletson is to compare his innings after lunch with one played for England *v* Central Zone:

ALLETSON at Hove, 20 May 1911		BOTHAM at Indore, 21 January 1982
142	Runs	122
40	Time (minutes)	55
51	Balls	55
8	6s	7
18	4s	16
2	3s	–
6	2s	3
4	1s	10
12	Not scored from	19
278	Runs/100 balls	221
152	Partnership	137
10* Riley	Partner	10* Gatting
70	Balls	75
217	Runs/100 balls	182
17.3	Over rate per hour	13.4

In their second innings – requiring 237 to win, Sussex finished on 213 for 8.

Modern cricketers who seek to emulate Alletson's innings will seek an answer to the question – 'What did Alletson have for lunch?'

15

It Won't Happen Again - 1

The Honourable Lionel (later Lord) Tennyson could never remember if he had engaged one Walter Livsey as his gentleman's personal gentleman and then ordered him to keep wicket for Hampshire, or if he had – as it were – plucked him from behind the stumps to act as his gentleman's personal gentleman. Of one thing the Hon. Lionel was certain: that his grandfather Alfred, Lord Tennyson had written the poem *Hiawatha*, a work attributed by everyone else to Henry Wadsworth Longfellow. The Hon. Lionel Tennyson's favourite drink was champagne.

When he awoke on 14 June 1922, Tennyson asked Livsey where he was.

'At Edgbaston, my lord. Today we shall begin a match with Warwickshire.'

The sun was shining. On reaching the County ground, Tennyson found the pitch to be perfect. As Livsey ran his bath (which would enable him to perspire and exude the previous night's champagne) Tennyson won the toss from Warwickshire's captain, the Hon. F. S. G. Calthorpe, and put his opponents in to bat.

'Inform Hampshire, Livsey, that we are fielding. I have decided to skittle Warwickshire and then bat until the close of play tomorrow.'

Livsey raised an eyebrow, then prepared the Hon. Lionel's morning stimulant.

Hampshire did not skittle Warwickshire, they merely dismissed them by four o'clock for 223. Reminding his men they were to bat until 6.30 the following evening, the Hon. Lionel then partook of another stimulant.

Hampshire made a poor start, Tennyson going in at 0 for 3 wickets. After he had scored a lusty boundary stroke which seemed to bounce from the head of mid-off, the score was soon 5 for 4 wickets. There was something of a middle order collapse, whereupon Livsey placed another stimulant before his employer, and reached for his bat.

'Where are you going, Livsey?'

'To the wicket, my lord.'

'Then I command you to hold the fort.'

'I will do my best to give satisfaction, my lord.'

Livsey's first act at the crease was to obscure the Warwickshire wicketkeeper and so acquire 4 byes. His second act was to miss a straight ball.

HAMPSHIRE – First Innings

A. Bowell	b Howell	0
A. Kennedy	c Smith b Calthorpe	0
H. L. V. Day	b Calthorpe	0
C. P. Mead	not out	6
Hon. L. H. Tennyson	c Calthorpe b Howell	4
G. Brown	b Howell	0
J. Newman	c C. Smart b Howell	0
W. R. Shirley	c J. Smart b Calthorpe	1
A. S. McIntyre	lbw, b Calthorpe	0
W. H. Livsey	b Howell	0
G. S. Boyes	lbw, b Howell	0
Extras (B 4)		4
Total		15

Fall of wickets: 1–0, 2–0, 3–0, 4–5, 5–5, 6–9, 7–10, 8–10, 9–15, 10–15

WARWICKSHIRE BOWLING – First Innings

	O.	M.	R.	W.
H. Howell	4.5	2	7	6
F. S. G. Calthorpe	4	3	4	4

Tennyson took pride in his boundary stroke, and congratulated Livsey on obscuring the wicketkeeper.

'But for our combined efforts, Livsey, Hampshire would have been dismissed for 7. Mr Calthorpe now informs me he wishes us to bat again.'

Tennyson also mentioned that various Warwickshire members had laid long odds against Hampshire winning the game.

By close of play on the first day, Hampshire were 98 for 3 wickets in their second innings – still 110 in arrears.

Thursday, 15 June was another fine day.

'Livsey, what did I decide we should do today?'

'Bat until the close of play, my lord.'

By lunch, Hampshire had lost Mead, Tennyson and Newman. With only 4 second-innings wickets to fall, they were still 34 behind. The Hon. Lionel Tennyson announced he was displeased with his team's progress.

'Gad! There's Mead eating pickles. Livsey, how can a man eat pickles at a time like this?'

'Mead is a left-hander, my lord.'

At 274 Hampshire's eighth wicket fell, their lead a mere 66. As Livsey prepared to leave the pavilion, Tennyson said he did not wish to see his gentleman's personal gentleman again until close of play.

'And that goes for Brown, too.'

George Brown was a gifted all-rounder. The previous summer he had opened the batting and kept wicket for England against Warwick Armstrong's Australians. Sometimes he opened the bowling for Hampshire. A man of immense strength, Brown liked to annoy fast bowlers by permitting short-pitched deliveries to hit his chest. He then leered and said, 'Yah!' At Edgbaston on 15 June 1922 he was in fine form. His partnership with Livsey lasted 140 minutes and realized 177 runs before he was out for 172. As Hampshire left the field on 475 for 9 wickets – Livsey 81 not out – the Hon. Lionel Tennyson nodded approval.

'Did I not say, Livsey, that Hampshire would skittle Warwickshire and then bat until 6.30 on the second day?'

'You did indeed, my lord.'

On Friday, 16 June 1922, Livsey completed his century and was undefeated when Hampshire's last wicket fell. After the unsuccessful first innings, the scorecard was remarkable.

HAMPSHIRE – Second Innings

A. Bowell	c Howell b W. G. Quaife	45
A. Kennedy	b Calthorpe	7
H. L. V. Day	c Bates b W. G. Quaife	15
C. P. Mead	b Howell	24
Hon. L. H. Tennyson	c C. Smart b Calthorpe	45
G. Brown	b C. Smart	172
J. Newman	c & b W. G. Quaife	12
W. R. Shirley	lbw, b Fox	30
A. S. McIntyre	lbw, b Howell	5
W. H. Livsey	not out	110
G. S. Boyes	b Howell	29
Extras (B 14, LB 11, W 1, NB 1)		27
Total		521

Fall of wickets: 1–15, 2–63, 3–81, 4–127, 5–152, 6–177, 7–262, 8–274, 9–451, 10–521

WARWICKSHIRE BOWLING – Second Innings

	O.	M.	R.	W.
H. Howell	63	10	156	3
F. S. G. Calthorpe	33	7	97	2
W. G. Quaife	49	8	154	3
J. Fox	13	2	30	1
J. Smart	13	2	37	0
F. R. Santall	5	0	15	0
C. Smart	1	0	5	1

Informing his men they would now dismiss Warwickshire right speedily, Tennyson led them on to the field. Alec Kennedy and Jack Newman took 9 wickets between them: Warwickshire 158. Hampshire had won by 155 runs.

Tennyson's winnings were considerable; that evening the whole Hampshire side drank champagne.

It won't happen again. English county captains no longer employ gentlemen's personal gentlemen as wicketkeeper–batsmen – nor wicketkeeper–batsmen as gentlemen's personal gentlemen.

16

Hobbs and Sutcliffe

The ideal opening pair must both be great batsmen, equally at ease on hard or green, on crumbling or sticky wickets. They must regard fast bowling with equanimity, swing as a mathematical proposition to be solved by logic, and spin as a problem (for batsmen have feet) valid only in the bowler's mind. They must be safe runners between the wickets, each must be supremely aware of his own, and his partner's, mastery. Such a pair once existed.

John Berry Hobbs of Surrey and Herbert Sutcliffe of Yorkshire were the greatest opening pair in history. They first appeared for England together in 1924 when their respective ages were forty-one and twenty-nine, and continued until the close of the 1930 season. In twenty-four Tests against Australia, South Africa and West Indies (another, at Trent Bridge in 1926, was washed out after half an hour when they were still in possession) only once when England batted twice did they fail to oblige with a partnership of at least 50.

In twenty-four Tests they had a century partnership on fifteen occasions.

Hobbs, of course, had seen everything before he met Sutcliffe. As a young man he had begun his Test career against Australia in 1907–8; over the next few years his partners were F. L. Fane, George Gunn, A. C. MacLaren, C. B. Fry, Tom Hayward and Septimus Kinneir. Then, during the tour of South Africa in 1909–10, he was joined by one who had gone in last for England a decade earlier – Wilfred Rhodes. Before the Great War intervened, the 'firm' of Hobbs and Rhodes had opened a Test match innings twenty-eight times with an average of 70. Eight century partnerships, with 323 against

Australia at Melbourne in 1911–12, marked this stage of Hobbs's career.

Learie Constantine once said that the great professional English batsmen of the inter-war years reached their peak at thirty-five and maintained it for the next seven years, so great was their technical skill. Hobbs was a case in point: after entering his fortieth year, he scored 108 first-class hundreds. In 1928 he was forty-five – thereafter he played 258 innings with an average of 59, and 51 hundreds. The difference between the young and the old Hobbs was that he went increasingly on to the back foot; having first set out to destroy bowling, he was later content to tame it. The outcome was the same. The great Australian Stanley McCabe once described the most valuable coaching he had ever received. It consisted of watching Hobbs's footwork against a decidedly fast Wall, and the wiles of Grimmett, in the Trent Bridge Test of 1930 when the batsman was aged forty-seven.

Herbert Sutcliffe did not recognize bowlers. That is to say, he did not believe there was any bowler capable of dismissing him. Bill O'Reilly once beat him several times in an over. Said the outraged bowler, 'He just stood there leering at me!' Although Sutcliffe had all the strokes, opponents argued he used but three. But which three? That depended upon the bowling and Sutcliffe's mood. For the greater glory of Yorkshire or England, he would make a six-hour hundred; he was also capable of hitting 10 sixes in an innings, and (with little more than token support from Leyland) striking 75 runs in 4 overs from Kenneth Farnes. One way or another, Herbert Sutcliffe was a very remarkable person.

His first Test excursion with Hobbs was successful – 136 together against South Africa at Edgbaston in 1924, England making 438 on the opening day. On the second the tourists' manager arrived late at the ground and beamed at a scoreboard showing 50 without loss. It was gently pointed out to him that South Africa were following on – Arthur Gilligan and Tate having caused a first-innings collapse of some magnitude: 75 deliveries, 10 wickets, 30 runs. Extras totalled 11, a gift of some proportions*.

The Lord's Test saw the enthronement of our heroes. On Saturday South Africa made 273, and England 28 for none. At lunch on Monday, after an eleven o'clock start, the score was

* A similar proportion by the close on 28 December 1926 would have seen Victoria 1,107 all out, Extras 405. It sounds even better as Sundries 405.

228 for none, both batsmen past a century. The partnership came to an end at 268 when Sutcliffe played on for 122 – the rate of progress 80 an hour. Because we are here concerned only with two opening batsmen, we shall merely whisper that No. 3 was Frank Woolley, that he and Hobbs added 142 at nearly 2 runs a minute, that Hobbs went for 211, and England finally declared at 531 for 2. A disappointing South African side: no real practice for 1924–5 tour of Australia. The bowlers there would soon find the weak spots.

They did – but not until Hobbs and Sutcliffe had put their signatures on the series. 157 and 110 were their first-wicket partnerships in the First Test at Sydney; already their running between the wickets was remarkable. Wilfred Rhodes had taken the hint long before: 'When Jack runs, I run.' So, too, with Sutcliffe. Hobbs's method of disturbing the fielders was simple: a full swing of the bat as though promising a drive, a last minute adjustment so that the stroke was checked, and the ball trickled a few yards. Fielders as agile as Tommy Andrews and Vic Richardson could do nothing to prevent singles when Hobbs was at the crease.

At Melbourne in the next Test Australia batted for two days in making 600. Hobbs and Sutcliffe decided on a gesture. They first rebuked, then chastised Jack Gregory, Charles Kelleway, Mailey and Arthur Richardson: at the close of the third day England were 283 for no wicket. Two hundreds in the match for Sutcliffe meant three in succession; the pair looked so impregnable that only one question remained to be answered – How good would they be on a sticky wicket? Did they have the techniques to conquer when conditions were wholly in favour of bowlers?

Occasionally a batsman had triumphed in such circumstances. At Melbourne in 1903–4 torrential rain was followed by a hot sun: England's first innings subsided from 279 for 3 to 315 all out, Australia made 122, England batted again for 103, and Australia tottered to 111. But one batsman on either side thumbed his nose. In Australia's first innings the scorecard read

74, 10, 5, 0, 1, 18, 2, 1, 8, 0, 2 not out.

Victor Trumper dealt with the situation. So did Johnny Tyldesley when it was England's turn: 3, 0, 62, 3, 0, 4, 9, 0, 10 not out, 4 – with one man absent ill. But never had a sticky wicket produced two great innings by the same team.

On 17 August 1926 Hobbs and Sutcliffe wrought their first Test match miracle. M. A. Noble, who was present, regarded it as a con-trick of the highest class. When play started, England were 49 for none (Hobbs 28, Sutcliffe 20) in their second innings, just 27 runs ahead. The previous night a thunderstorm had broken over south London; how long before the sun came out and turned the Oval wicket into a genuine sticky? The answer was about an hour, by which time England were 80. Arthur Richardson then appeared with off-spin, four short-legs and a short mid-on. At the end of 10 overs – 8 of them taken by Hobbs – a single had been added to the score.

The ball jumped up at every angle; each was dropped at the batsman's feet. But where were the batsman's feet? Hobbs took guard almost twelve inches outside his leg stump, moving quickly into position as he noted the ball's length and direction. Anything that popped harmlessly, he allowed to hit him. Each ball took a piece of turf as it pitched; Hobbs removed the bits after anaesthetizing the biting spin. In Richardson's eleventh over, he raised the siege, hitting a 2 and a 4. Meanwhile Sutcliffe batted with an eye on eternity – for this was a timeless Test.

In two and a half hours before lunch, England made 112 – Hobbs 69 and Sutcliffe 33. The Master was within three runs of his century which he got immediately after the interval, with a stroke off Gregory which went a few yards. Then he was bowled: 172–1–100. Sutcliffe stayed until the day's last over, for 161, and England won easily, so regaining the Ashes. But why, asked Noble, had not the Australian captain, Collins, attacked during the morning with Macartney and himself – bowlers whose left-arm spin made the ball leave the bat? Hobbs had only *pretended* to find difficulty in Richardson. When taxed with this assertion, the batsman smiled and said nothing.

An Oval sticky in the days of uncovered wickets was nothing compared to a Melbourne beast. Yet in January 1929, when England were set 332 to win – and great bowlers of the past like Hugh Trumble said they would be lucky to make 70 – Hobbs and Sutcliffe again did their incredible party piece. At Melbourne the pitch deteriorated so completely that the England captain would not risk a roller of any kind. But Hobbs and Sutcliffe coped with balls that lifted shoulder-high, with balls that crept, with balls that turned almost at right angles. 105 for the first wicket – Hobbs 49. Sutcliffe lasted for 7 hours and 135; England won by 3 wickets. This was just one of the occasions when the great Yorkshireman contemplated a vile pitch, and said there was no problem – 'So long as Jack didn't get out.'

Hobbs and Sutcliffe were legends long before they retired, their record for first wicket partnerships of over 100 runs:

Hobbs with partner 166 Sutcliffe with partner 145
Hobbs and Sutcliffe 26
(15 in Tests)

Sometimes Sutcliffe was content to play second fiddle. Lancashire were County champions in 1928, and at the close of the season played the Rest of England. The spearhead of the champions' attack was the awesome Australian, Ted Macdonald, as dangerous as Larwood. The Rest's first wicket fell after 140 minutes:

J. B. Hobbs	c Sibbles	b Hopwood	150
H. Sutcliffe	not out		54
Extras			8
			212

Hobbs was in frisky mood, hooking Macdonald's bouncers repeatedly to the boundary. When the bowler fired at the off-stump, Hobbs took a pace back and cut him high over the slips. Sutcliffe, of course, made his hundred; he was playing with undue care in order to reach 3,000 runs for the season.

17

It Happened

Harold Larwood was quick, and Maurice Tate was certainly no slouch: certainly when either hit a batsman on the thigh, he was apt to hop about. Both played for England in the Lord's Test of 1926.

We now call upon photographic evidence:

1. Although Herbert Strudwick stood up to Tate (as his successor Duckworth did, as Tiger Smith had to Barnes, and Godfrey Evans would to Alec Bedser), he was back a very long way to Larwood. Therefore we may assume the wicket was not slow.

2. Warren Bardsley, a left-hander, and Bill Woodfull, a right-hander, walked to the middle each with a glove on his bottom hand. The top hand was unprotected against a bowler of Larwood's pace.

3. Jack Gregory batted, as always, without a glove on either hand.

The question is not whether the batsmen were certifiable, but how they knew they would not be hit on the top hand or, in Gregory's case, either hand.

18

A Mighty Midget

Alfred Percy Freeman was a late developer. Not in size, for he stopped growing a couple of inches over five feet – hence 'Tich' Freeman. But he was a late developer in the exploitation of his skills.

Aged thirty, his first-class wickets totalled 29. This was strange in that Freeman would become the second most prolific of all wicket-takers: 3,776 to the 4,187 of Wilfred Rhodes. At the age of thirty, the great Yorkshireman had already dismissed 1,934 batsmen.

So, in the fourth decade of his life, Freeman set about refining his skills – the most beguiling and delectable of all in cricket. Trotting up to the crease with apparently bland indifference, he dispensed leg-breaks and googlies. Flight and spin were so artfully woven that batsmen began to succumb. But not altogether convulsively. Between the ages of thirty-one and thirty-nine Freeman averaged only 150 wickets an English season.

Now was the time, not for retirement, but for supreme mastery. In eight years – 1928–35 – Freeman took 2,090 wickets at an average of 17.85, a wicket every 40 balls. To put this feat in perspective, and to show how cricket has altered over half a century, we must compare the mean of Freeman's eight golden summers with a representative one, 1981, from the present. Since Freeman's basic movement was away from a right-handed batsman, we shall compare him with three bowlers of similar movement, and also with three who come into the bat.

1928–35, av. per year.	Freeman	261 wkts at 17.85	Balls/wkt 40
1981	Underwood, Intikhab & Edmunds	216 wkts at 24.01,	BW 62
	Hemmings, Ackfield & Emburey	239 wkts at 22.40,	B/W 59

It will be pointed out that long before 1981 the emphasis had shifted to seam bowling, that we should be comparing Freeman with three men who headed the first-class averages in 1981 – Hadlee, Clarke and Garner (none of them born in England). Whereas Freeman's balls per wicket figure was 40, that of those three bowlers combined was 41. Perhaps *they* should be compared with the Larwood of 1931–2 when that terror was at his peak. 291 wickets at 12.49, balls per wicket *31*.

Perhaps it's time we changed the nature of English pitches.

Freeman's most absurd season was 1928. He took his 100th wicket on 22 June, his 200th on 27 July and his 300th on 14 September. Meanwhile, from behind the stumps for Kent, Leslie Ames looked on impassively and reacted when necessary – 121 victims: 69 catches and 52 stumpings. Wise men did not play back to Freeman for his top-spinner was lethal; they went forward, sometimes dragging the back foot, or went down the pitch. Ames was ready.

On 9, 11 and 12 June, Kent played Sussex at Tunbridge Wells. After Kent had made 237, Freeman and another leg-spinner, C. S. Marriott, opened the bowling. Kent's victory was less amazing than the identity of their destroyers:

Freeman & Marriott	123.4–28–294–19
3 other bowlers	27–6–82–1

Here it must be admitted that Freeman was Kent's only regular bowler of class. So the inevitability of his success was, in a way, assured. BUT Kent came second in the County Championship, a happening which – if we denigrate the skills of Freeman – takes some explaining away.

From time to time some quick-footed batsman would get after Freeman and 'murder' him. However, in 1928 he bamboozled such masters as Hammond, Hendren, Hobbs, Mead, Sandham and Sutcliffe. The moral is clear: a bowler who reaches the age of thirty with only 29 wickets in first-class cricket must not be discouraged.

19

It Won't Happen Again-2

At 11.45 on the morning of 27 December 1926, McNamee of New South Wales bowled a no-ball to the Victorian opener Ponsford. Although the batsman mis-cued his stroke, this proved to be the most expensive no-ball in cricket history. McNamee, a man with a keen sense of humour, found the immediate aftermath of his no-ball funny. Before long, ten other New South Welshmen were glowering at McNamee; the next day they took his name in vain.

Of course, New South Wales should have done better than totter to 221 all out on the first day of this game at Melbourne (that was Friday, 24 December). Had they known what was about to happen, they would have been well advised to forgo the Saturday's Christmas dinner, in which case Sunday's sleeping off of same would not have been necessary.

When Victoria began their reply on Monday morning, the two Bills – Woodfull and Ponsford – seemed in good form. At this stage of his illustrious career, William Maldon Woodfull was known as the 'Unbowlable'. William Harold Ponsford was bowlable but only after he had made 200 or so. The sensible way to dismiss either was by a run-out, but as both were responsible citizens who regarded their fellow men with suspicion, run-outs were rare.

With Victoria on 17, McNamee was guilty of a no-ball. Ponsford played a short-arm pull but mis-cued; instead of 4 to mid-wicket, the ball lobbed into the hands of the New South Wales captain, Alan Kippax, at mid-on. Instead of being 21 for 0, the score was still 17 for 0. Suddenly the crowd realized it was about to be 17 for 1. Woodfull had called Ponsford for a single (off a no-ball!) and was in the middle of the pitch. Ponsford roared 'No! Go back!'

Woodfull did not go back, there was no point in it. For Kippax was lobbing the ball gently and accurately into McNamee's hands as he stood over the bowler's stumps. However, as the ball reached McNamee, the intended recipient not only tripped over the stumps but fell flat on his face. With the ball some distance from McNamee, Woodfull got the message and scrambled home. Three and a half hours later, he was caught at the wicket.

Victoria 375 for 1. Last man 133.

So far the scoring rate had been exactly 100 an hour; by the close Ponsford and Hunter Hendry had increased it to 106.

VICTORIA

W. M. Woodfull	c Ratcliffe b Andrews	133
W. H. Ponsford	not out	334
H. L. Hendry	not out	86
Extras		30
Total (one wicket)		573

The New South Wales bowling figures were not very interesting. The great googly bowler Arthur Mailey (at this stage 28–0–148–0) always contended that Ponsford played spin better than any man living, a verdict accepted even by those who spent hours attacking Bradman.

On Tuesday, 28 December a goodly crowd of 22,348 assembled to watch Ponsford beat Clem Hill's Sheffield Shield record score of 365 not out. What they saw, however, was a Victoria collapse of sorts. This was really the fault of Hendry, who gave his wicket away.

594–2–100.

Ponsford was still 13 short of Hill's record when he snicked a ball on to his foot and thence on to his stumps. Saying with some feeling, 'By cripes, I am unlucky!' Ponsford departed. True, he had scored at almost a run a minute, but he had promised himself to bat for two whole days. The following season – after Queensland had put Victoria in – he was again disappointed, 437 coming in just short of two days.

614–3–352.

Victoria's collapse of sorts continued, both Love and King being stumped off Mailey.

631–4–6 and 657–5–7.

But Ryder and Hartkopf brought about a recovery. Playing each ball on its merits, they added 177 in an hour and a half before Hartkopf, too, was deceived by Mailey.

834–6–61.

Meanwhile Ryder, whose first century had come in 115 minutes, now accelerated to a second in 74 minutes. When Liddicut was out, the recovery was complete.

915–7–36.

With Ellis as partner, Ryder dominated the proceedings. However, the sight of 1,000 on the board caused him (as it would have caused any batsman not born in Yorkshire) to grow over-confident. On 275 he faced Andrews, and hit the first 4 balls of the over for 4, 6, 4, 6. Deciding to reach 300 with a drive over the Stand, Ryder skied a catch to Kippax. He had made his last 95 runs in 56 minutes. Ryder's innings had been played at 72 runs an hour.

1,043–8–295.

Morton, the Victoria fast bowler, marched in. Without more ado he ran himself out.

1,046–9–0. Morton liked to forget this match. The other twenty-one players who took part in it either scored at least one run or took a wicket. Morton took no wicket and scored no run.

Blackie, Victoria's No. 11, was a fine off-spinner whose ideas of batting were rudimentary. But now he discovered the ball hitting the middle of his bat, a sign the bowlers were tiring. Suddenly he and Ellis found themselves at the same end of the wicket. Loudly they disagreed about the possibility of a run. At mid-wicket Andrews wondered whether to shy at the bowler's stumps or to send in a gentle lob. Remembering Kippax some ten and a quarter hours and 1,090 runs earlier, Andrews ran to the bowler's end and whipped off the bails.

1,107–10–63.

Victoria's run rate had fallen from 106 an hour on the first day to 102 an hour on the second. Mailey was disappointed when the last wicket fell – 'Just as I was finding my length.'

NEW SOUTH WALES 221 (N. E. Phillips 52) and 230 (A. A. Jackson 59 not out; Hartkopf 6 for 98).

VICTORIA

W. M. Woodfull	c Radcliffe	b Morgan	133
W. H. Ponsford	b Morgan		352
H. L. Hendry	c Morgan	b Mailey	100
J. S. Ryder	c Kippax	b Andrews	295
H. S. Love	st Radcliffe	b Mailey	6
S. King	st Radcliffe	b Mailey	7
A. E. V. Hartkopf	c McGuirk	b Mailey	61
A. E. Liddicut	b McGuirk		36
J. L. Ellis	run out		63
F. L. Morton	run out		0
D. J. Blackie	not out		27
Extras			27
Total			1,107

New South Wales Bowling

	O.	M.	R.	W.
R. McNamee	24	2	124	0
H. McGuirk	26	1	130	1
A. A. Mailey	64	0	362	4
N. Campbell	11	0	89	0
N. E. Phillips	11.7	0	64	0
G. Morgan	26	0	137	1
T. J. E. Andrews	21	2	148	2
A. F. Kippax	7	0	26	0

VICTORIA WON BY AN INNINGS AND 656 RUNS

And why won't something like the above match ever happen again? Because bowling has improved and scientifically placed fields make scoring difficult? No. Because during this run riot New South Wales averaged 144 balls an hour.

While Victoria scored at more than 100 runs an hour – and did so for two whole days, New South Wales averaged the equivalent of 24 *six-ball overs an hour*.

It won't happen again.

20

Donald George Bradman

During Bradman's first tour of England in 1930 he made 58 against Glamorgan. Next day newspaper placards read

BRADMAN FAILS!

To appreciate the absurdity of the man we must play with figures. We may conclude that his fame is over-rated; we shall do so only by insisting that none of his contemporaries could bowl.

Bradman played 338 first-class innings.

In 221 of these he did not make a century. They averaged 58.20. Now let us see this 58.20 in perspective. It was a higher average than that achieved (*with their century innings included*) by such batsmen as Ranjitsinhji and C. B. Fry, Jack Hobbs and Walter Hammond, in our own time by Sobers and Boycott, Barry Richards and Vivian Richards. So Bradman was not altogether unsuccessful, even when he missed a three-figure score.

Neville Cardus thought that Bradman should automatically have been given out on reaching 100. Had the laws of cricket permitted this, his 338 first-class innings would have averaged 61.64.

It is time to consider the sheer awfulness of Bradman and the occasions when he made a century:

117 innings over 100: average 216.48
37 innings over 200: average 314.80
6 innings over 300: average 539.00

As the laws of cricket did not oblige Bradman to retire after reaching his century, the career average of this unique batsman was 95.14.

In Test matches he played 80 innings with an average of 99.94. He was more likely to make a century, or double century, in Tests than in other first-class games:

29 innings over 100: average 234.47
12 innings over 200: average 275.72

Against England he twice passed 300 in an innings.

Wilfred Rhodes, Harold Larwood, Alec Bedser and Jim Laker had combined careers stretching from 1898 to 1964. Between them they bowled at everyone from W. G. Grace, Ranjitsinhji, Victor Trumper, Jack Hobbs, Charles Macartney, Walter Hammond and Bill Ponsford to Neil Harvey, Worrell, Weekes and Walcott. They had one thing in common; asked the name of the greatest batsman they tried to dismiss, they all replied 'Bradman!'

The England–Australian Test at Lord's in 1930 had everything. To many it was the ideal game of cricket. It was, incidentally, the first four-day Test to be played at headquarters – something which England tended to overlook before things got underway. Winning the toss on a perfect wicket, England made 405 for 9 on the first day. Frank Woolley, opening in place of an injured Sutcliffe, casually drove and flicked 41 runs off 46 balls before being miraculously caught by Tim Wall in the gully. Duleepsinhji then made 173 in his first game against Australia. By the close of the second day Australia had replied to England's 425 with 404 for 2. Declaring on the third afternoon at 729 for 6, Australia fielded to an England second innings of 375 (a wonderful 121 from Percy Chapman*), before going on to win by 7 wickets. 1,601 runs in less than four days!

This was the occasion of what Bradman always regarded as his finest innings. Of course he had the advantage of starting after Woodfull and Ponsford had worn down the England bowling in a partnership of 162 – apparently a tedious affair which took nearly three hours. Bradman arrived at 3.30 to face the bowling of J. C. White, a left-hander of legendary accuracy. Eighteen months previously in Australia, White had repeatedly contained batsmen – so much so that Jack Ryder, the Australian captain, described him as England's key bowler in spite of the presence of Larwood, Tate and Geary.

* An innings easily summed up as one played by a left-handed Botham – K.G.

But this was 28 June 1930. To White's first ball, naturally of impeccable length, Bradman went yards down the wicket and drove it to long-off. The murder of England had begun, Bradman batting as though he already had a century to his name. When he played a defensive stroke, it was consummate in its cold precision; generally he shattered the bowling with every shot imaginable, most devastating of all his pull to mid-wicket. His 50 came in 45 minutes from 56 balls; he then waited upon Woodfull till tea while that batsman reached 100.

Australia 244 for 1 at the 4.30 interval, Bradman 54. The 46 runs to Bradman's century now came in 45 minutes; thereafter, in the hour before the close he cruised, making 55. On the third day Bradman's innings ended at 254 when, for the first time, he lofted a ball. Chapman's catch in the covers was amazing even for him. However, the cautious reader may argue that Bradman's success at Lord's was due in part to his coming in to face tiring bowlers. Perhaps it was.

A fortnight later at Leeds the third Test began. This time Australia won the toss only to lose Archie Jackson in the second over of the day. 2–1–1. On paper at least, England was playing a stronger attack – Larwood having replaced Gubby Allen, Dick Tyldesley and George Geary Walter Robins and White. At all events it was an attack harder to score from, Tyldesley's length as a leg-spinner more reliable than that of Robins. Things did not work out in the prescribed way for England.

With the Australian score 2 for 1, England had an attacking field. This accounted for the fact that Bradman scored faster before lunch than in either of the two later sessions. At lunch he was 105 made at 56 runs an hour, at tea 220 and at the close 309 – the hourly run rate since lunch only fractionally over 50. Bradman finished the day quite fresh, the bowlers less so. It is time to pay tribute to those bowlers – Allen and Larwood fast, Tate, Hammond and Geary medium-pace, White, Robins and Tyldesley slow.

During the 1930 season they conceded in all matches 36 runs every 100 balls, their collective average was 19.40. But in the Lord's and Leeds Test matches *in only two innings*, they were struck for 539 runs by Bradman – 70 runs coming from every 100 balls. At the end of the five Tests, during which he scored 974 runs, Bradman had travelled at 61 runs per 100 balls; Duleepsinhji and Hammond, England's fastest scoring regular batsmen, at 40 runs per 100 balls. Except that Australia possessed Grimmett, England had the stronger bowling side. In short, Bradman had revolutionized cricket; he could score fast without taking risks.

Some will shrug and say, 'But Bradman played in an age of batsmen's pitches.' True. And so did his contemporaries. But no one ever looked like rivalling his achievements. His footwork was so remarkable that the definition of a good length ball had to be revised when he was batting. He seemed capable of forcing deliveries of almost any length. His self-confidence was, to bowlers, appalling; it did not occur to Bradman that anyone could get him out. The England captain of 1932–3, Douglas Jardine, knew better; he would restrict Bradman with 'bodyline' bowling.

This consisted of Larwood – whose accuracy and pace were alike phenomenal – pitching short of a length on the leg stump, with as many as six short-legs in attendance and two long-legs awaiting the brave hook shot. Bradman's reaction may be ignored; not those of Victor Richardson, bravest of the brave and grandfather of Ian and Greg Chappell. 'When I took leg-stump guard, the ball came straight for me. I moved a foot outside the leg stump and the ball still came straight for me.' The new form of attack reduced Bradman to normal terms; in eight innings he averaged only 56, a figure superior to that of England's Sutcliffe and Hammond who were not facing 'bodyline'. Failure!

The Bradman of 1930 had disappeared for ever. Four years later in England, and in fitful health (just after the end of the tour he was operated on for an almost gangrenous appendix), he fluctuated between the rashly impetuous and the even more blindingly brilliant. Two hundred and seventy-one in a day at Leeds was, until the final hour, a defensive effort which took Australia from 39 for 3 to 494 for 4. Things looked up at the Oval when his 244 came at almost 90 runs per 100 balls. And so on into immortality – a trite statement considering that Bradman had become immortal by the age of twenty-one.

Bradman today would, of course, be another matter. The current over-rates would presumably make 200 in a day his maximum effort. On the other hand, bearing in mind Wilfred Rhodes's tribute – 'Bradman were good bat. Best bat Ah ever saw – off back foot' and the modern short of a length bowling, it is hard to see how he might have got out.

21

Case

Cecil Charles Cowper Case played for Somerset between the wars. He was more familiarly known as 'Box' or 'C^4'. A solicitor by profession, Case was a suspicious man; when he signed his autograph, his pen moved slowly as though fearful of providing too many, or too few, Cs. Being bald, Case always wore a cap, an article presumably once new but grown faded and wrinkled.

Case was an original. Once he was the recipient of a vicious bouncer from William Voce. A bouncer from Voce called for thought and often evasive action, even if your name was Bradman. Case took what he thought was evasive action but knocked down his stumps and lost his bat. Having recovered, he prepared to depart in bemused dudgeon. So, picking up a stump, he tucked it under his arm. He had walked some distance before a Notts fielder gently informed Case of the situation, and substituted bat for stump.

But Case also played the stroke of the century. It was against Lancashire at Old Trafford. The pitch was wet, Case's feet heavy with anxiety. At the sight of a top-spinner from the vast and rubicund Dick Tyldesley, Case opted to play forward. However, something in the mechanism of the stroke went awry. Case fell flat on his face yet – mark the YET – contrived to stop Tyldesley's top-spinner with bat held an inch or two before his face. Thinking for a moment that he had secured the first 'head-before-wicket' of his life, the bowler appealed. The umpire shook his head, Case raised his – and the game continued.

22

Steadfast

In the autumn of 1930 an MCC party left for South Africa under the captaincy of Percy Chapman. If not wholly representative, it was far from negligible, including as it did Bob Wyatt, Sandham, Hammond, Hendren, Leyland, Tate, Voce, Peebles and J. C. White. As usual, there were two wicketkeepers, but they made strange reading to many when the team was announced:

G. Duckworth (Lancashire)
W. Farrimond (Lancashire)

Some in the south of England asked 'W. Who?' How can you have two wicketkeepers from the same county? Ridiculous. Not really. Bill Farrimond was a brilliant wicketkeeper who first appeared for his county in 1924 during a Test match where Duckworth was officiating. Thereafter he was stand-in for George, playing two Tests in South Africa for Chapman's team, and one in 1935 at Lord's when Ames was in the same side for his batting. Aged thirty-five in 1938, Farrimond took over for Lancashire on Duckworth's retirement and kept for two seasons. Many times other counties approached him with offers: Farrimond wouldn't leave his beloved Lancashire.

In 1931 Hedley Verity took 138 wickets for Yorkshire in the Championship, Arthur Booth took one when Verity was playing for England. Any chance of promotion blocked by Verity, Booth drifted away to bowl slow left-arm for Northumberland. Years passed; Verity was killed in the Second World War; Yorkshire at the start of the 1946 season looked about for a left-arm bowler. They found one – Arthur Booth, aged forty-three. There were quite a few good bowlers of Booth's type around after the War: Jack Young of Middlesex,

'Sam' Cook of Gloucestershire, Dick Howorth of Worcestershire, James Langridge of Sussex, all of whom had played, or would play, for England. And who headed the national averages in 1946? Arthur Booth of Yorkshire with 111 wickets at 11.61.

His point made, Booth retired.

23

Bradman (continued)

The new ball is a fearsome thing. Bowlers who use the new ball must be treated with awe. The duty of opening batsmen is to survive the new ball and remove its shine so that those who follow may not be subjected to the late movement of the aforesaid fearsome thing. Opening batsmen are conditioned to deal with the new ball, mere stroke-players are not.

But when does a new ball cease to be new? Clearly, after an hour or two have passed with the scoring of 50 or 100 runs. All things being equal, a ball should still be definable as 'new' if only 10 runs have been scored from it.

Bradman played 80 innings in Test matches; on sixteen occasions he went in with 10 or fewer runs on the board. The average Australian total when Bradman was thus cast to the wolves was 4. A ball should still be new after only 4 runs have been scored from it. How did Bradman react to the fearsome object?

He removed the shine and flattened the seam by hitting the ball. On the sixteen occasions when he was, in effect, turned into an opening batsman, he averaged 108.53. He did not score fast, only at 41 runs an hour. So if he went in at, say, 11.40 on an English morning, his century arrived at 2.45.

The bowlers who contributed to this feat, and who were generally capable of using the new ball effectively, included Larwood, Tate, Voce, Bowes and 'Gubby' Allen of England, the West Indian Constantine, and the South African 'Sandy' Bell. Some of them could bowl.

Bradman made twelve double centuries in Test matches, 7 of them when going in with an average Australian score of 15 for 1.

During his first-class career, Bradman opened the innings only nine times with an average of 104.50.

The new ball is a fearsome thing.

24

Verity's Day

Hedley Verity was a tall, studious Yorkshireman whose greatest joy was bowling to Bradman on a perfect Australian pitch, taxing genius with a left-hander's classic line and length. At Adelaide in 1936–7 he sent down 37 8-ball overs for 54 runs while the almost inevitable double century took shape. On flawless turf a defensive master, Verity on a helpful wicket spat venom with the ball.

On 11 July 1932 Nottinghamshire stayed in all day at Headingley for 234, Verity 41–13–64–2. On the Monday Yorkshire slumped from 110 for 2 to 163 for 9 against a relentlessly accurate Larwood. Then a thunderstorm burst over the ground. Next day was sullen; Brian Sellars declared Yorkshire's innings 71 behind, play starting at 12.30. Nothing happened. Bowes at fast-medium had a few overs, Macaulay turned from seam to off-spin, Verity's problems were rational. At lunch Notts were 38, both Keeton and Shipston on 18.

Suddenly the sun broke through; the pitch cooked. Before lunch Verity had bowled to a solitary slip, now he had two. The ball turned sharply and lifted, six batsmen were caught by the wicketkeeper or in slips. Carr swung hopefully and found long-on exactly placed, Larwood skied the ball to extra-cover where Sutcliffe condescended to accept a difficult catch. Macaulay bowling round the wicket to short-legs was playable, Verity leaving the bat was not. The Notts scoresheet appeared thus:

W. W. Keeton	c Macaulay b Verity	21
F. W. Shipston	c Wood b Verity	21
W. Walker	c Macaulay b Verity	11
A. W. Carr	c Barber b Verity	0
A. Staples	c Macaulay b Verity	7
C. B. Harris	c Holmes b Verity	0
G. V. Gunn	lbw b Verity	0
B. Lilley	not out	3
H. Larwood	c Sutcliffe b Verity	0
W. Voce	c Holmes b Verity	0
S. J. Staples	st Wood b Verity	0
B 3, N–B 1		4
Total		67

Set 139 to win in 165 minutes, Yorkshire knocked off the runs with an hour to spare – Holmes not out 77, Sutcliffe not out 54. There was no one in the Notts side even remotely resembling Verity in method, let alone skill. The great bowler's analysis was perfect symmetry.

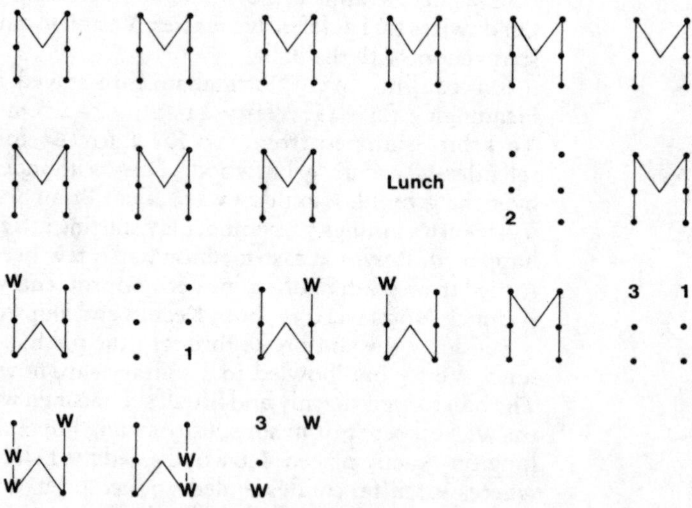

19.4 overs 16 maidens 10 runs 10 wickets

Captain Verity died at Caserta on 31 July 1943, of wounds received in battle.

25

Their Eyes Were Dim

Bespectacled bowlers are not a rarity. William Bowes of Yorkshire jogged professionally to the wicket before achieving a nasty and sharply rising out-swinger, Percy Mansell of South Africa spun from leg and the Australian Arthur Richardson the other way; Alfred Valentine passed 100 wickets for West Indies with slow left-arm guile before deciding he couldn't see without glasses. Percy Fender of Surrey and England (the greatest captain his country never had) donned and removed spectacles as the mood took him.

Perhaps the best-loved of all bowling spectacles men was Alec Skelding, a white-booted umpire with a nice line in patter. At 6.30 he was wont to remove the bails with a flourish and say, 'That concludes the entertainment for the day, gentlemen.' In earlier years, when bowling fastish for Leicestershire, he unburdened himself:

'The specs are there for the look of the thing. I can't see without 'em, and on hot days I can't see with 'em, as I'm bowling with steam in my eyes. So I do it on hearing only, and appeal twice an over.'

A pity Skelding never bowled when Skelding was umpire.

26

Definition

The ball bowled with what appears to be a leg-break action and turns from the off is variously known as the googly, the wrong 'un, the Bosie (after its inventor B. J. T. Bosanquet) – and epithets less friendly by its victims. Naturally it was a Somerset man, R. C. Robertson-Glasgow, who summed it up best: 'The ball that squints'.

27

Not Really About Bradman

Before lunch on 18 December 1948, the individual world record score belonged to Bradman – 452 not out *v* Queensland in 1929–30. Incidentally, a fortnight earlier Bradman had made his 117th and last first-class hundred: against Lindwall, Bill Johnston, Bruce Dooland and Colin McCool he had played himself in carefully (we quote from B. J. Wakley's monumental *Bradman the Great*) 'but nevertheless reached his 50 in an hour'. Now forget about Bradman.

Far away in India the Ranji Trophy games were in progress. These were played over four days until the semi-final, the authorities feeling that four days were at least sufficient for a decision on the first innings. On 16 December 1948 at Poona, Maharashtra began a match with Kathiawar who batted first. Although Thakur Saheb of Rajkot (as one might say Geoffrey Boycott of Fitzwilliam) made 77, Kathiawar were all out for 238. In due course they took a wicket with the Maharashtra score at 81; thereafter success eluded them for a while until – at 536 – K. V. Bhandarkar succumbed for 205.

He and B. B. Nimbalkar had added 455, so beating the world record second-wicket partnership set up by Ponsford and Bradman at the Oval in 1934 by 4 runs. Undismayed by this set-back, Maharashtra consolidated. As the score passed 600, then 700, and finally 800, it occurred to the men of Kathiawar that they were not going to win. By lunch on the third day, 18 December, Maharashtra were 826 for 4 – Nimbalkar 443 not out scored at 53 runs an hour. The lead was by then 588.

Eleven men of Kathiawar toyed with their lunch. They inspected their dudgeon which they found to be exceedingly high. The question was not whether Nimbalkar would beat Bradman's 452 but when: perhaps in 1 over, perhaps in 2. Then Kathiawar would be able to claim the distinction of having conceded the most runs by an individual batsman, so making Queensland feel happier.

'Right!' said the Kathiawar captain, 'We'll give up and go home.'

Victory was handed to Maharashtra on a plate, which was why after lunch on 18 December 1948 the record for the highest individual score was still held by D. G. Bradman.

28

The Incomparable

Garfield Sobers was not a greater left-hand batsman than Graeme Pollock. He was not a more devastating left-arm bowler with the new ball than Alan Davidson. His brilliance in the slips did not – could not – exceed that of Bobby Simpson. His catches at short-leg were not more miraculous than those of Davidson or Tony Lock. But translate all those negatives into positives and see what you are left with – a unique cricketer of genius.

Frankly, his presence in any side was unfair. Before each match the opposition should have been allowed to enter into negotiations:

'Do you wish Sobers to bat above No. 10 in the order? Because if so, he won't be permitted to bowl – *and* he'll field on the boundary. You want him to use the new ball? Later finger-spin, chinamen and googlies? Sorry! then he'll have to bat at No. 10. Made your mind up? Good! then let's get on with the game.'

The laws being what they were, Sobers constituted a problem. To see him emerge from the pavilion gave most bowlers a complex. Tall and well-built but not heavy, he gave the impression of cat-like power. Casual though controlled, he relaxed easily. If bowlers solved the problem of Sobers, batsmen felt dubious. An off-side snick from the bowling of Hall, a swoop by Sobers – a false stroke to the vicious late-swing of Sobers – a hard, low glance to short-leg from Gibbs's off-spin: whatever batsmen did, there was always a strong possibility that, as bowler or fielder, Sobers would ensnare them.

His pace with the new ball was deceptive. A run-up and

delivery suggested a fast-medium bowler. But a last minute effort in his action made the ball leave the pitch with uncommon zip, something much more than fast-medium. Added to which his left-hander's slant across the right-handed batsman presented an additional problem. Perhaps later in the same session of play, he would go round or over the wicket – his stock slow ball moving away from, or into, the right-hander. The new ball again available, Sobers re-measured his long run. Compelled by our imaginary law to go in No. 10 if allowed to bowl, Sobers would still have been an integral part of any West Indies side.

So, too, had his bowling been no better than that of some Aunt Jemima. Certain statistics are more vital than others; let us for a moment reduce Sobers to mere figures. Consider great batsmen who have ended their first-class careers with an average of 50 or more – and who were more successful in Tests than in lesser matches. The roll call is impressive: Bradman, Hammond, Hobbs, Hutton, Dudley Nourse, Sobers and Herbert Sutcliffe. Such was our incomparable's class as a specialist batsman.

Now recall where those Masters entered in the order: Hobbs, Hutton and Sutcliffe were openers, Bradman almost invariably came in at No. 3, and Hammond generally so, Dudley Nourse was a No. 4. In those positions the great batsmen were of supreme value to their teams. And Sobers? Well, it all depended. To begin with – when included as a slow bowler – he went in at No. 9 (once; he was then promoted). As a young man he sometimes opened, his average 50. Did first wicket down suit him better? No. 4 or No. 5? It didn't matter, he was at home anywhere. He was successful anywhere; whether he opened, or went in at 3, 4, 5 or 6, his Test average was 50 or more. 8,032 are a lot of runs.

They gave pleasure. The way they were made reduced strong men to drooling. Garfield Sobers was an attacking batsman. That is not to say his defence was weak, rather that his first thought was the subjugation of bowlers. This being so, it never occurred to him to wear a thigh-pad (if it did occur, he shook his head). A short-pitched ball on his body could be dealt with in various ways – fended down, forced for runs or hooked. Sobers liked to hook just behind square; occasionally, the stroke betrayed him, more often it brought 4 runs. Fred Trueman, never reluctant to soften up a batsman, rarely pitched short at Sobers. On one occasion Dennis Lillee mixed bouncers with yorkers; the former were hooked, the latter driven with savage contempt.

Two of the acutest brains in post-war cricket, Trevor Bailey and Ray Illingworth, pondered deeply over Sobers. Bailey, at fast-medium, found it disheartening when perfect length balls were struck for 4 without Sobers taking the slightest risk. The wily off-spinner Illingworth smiled wanly as he recalled, 'Gary getting a foot in the wrong place and then hitting the ball to the boundary off the middle of the bat.' Sobers not only saw the ball early, he could adjust later than mortal men.

A high back-lift and a full follow-through, strong wrists and perfect timing were the secrets of Sobers's power. The leg-stump ball flicked wide of mid-on, the off-stump delivery just short of a length and square cut as if with an axe, these were only two of the Sobers weapons of destruction. When the mood was on him, he played variations – the classical batsman indulged himself. Could he reach and drive that full-length ball on the off stump? He could – so he hit it past cover off the back foot. Did this in-swinger encourage dropped wrists and a single behind square-leg? Very well, then let's try . . . Once he dealt with such a ball by following it, and then driving to fine long-leg. Why not? Sobers saw the ball early, and adjusted late.

Was he as good as men recall? No. Bowlers at least were sure he was even better. Spectators regarded him as a supreme entertainer, one who welcomed – and accepted – a challenge. The Test record score of 365 not out was made by Sobers, the maximum runs – 36 – from a 6-ball over were extracted by Sobers; forget both feats save to acknowledge how fitting that both should have been wrought by a supremely great batsman. To watch Sobers for 10 minutes was more satisfying than enduring a century by So-and-so; the Grand Manner belonged by right to Sobers.

In 1950 Neville Cardus was invited by the BBC to broadcast a talk on his World XI of the century. Insisting the matches would be played over three days, Cardus suggested: Hobbs, Trumper, Bradman, Macartney, F. S. Jackson (captain), Aubrey Faulkner, Keith Miller, Rhodes, Oldfield, Larwood and S. F. Barnes. Twenty years later in conversation, Sir Neville brought his XI up to date: 'Jackson, I fear, must go. For how can we possibly ignore Sobers?'

29

R.C. R-G.

Draw up a short list of the finest cricket writers of all time, and you will place in the top three Raymond Charles Robertson-Glasgow – 'Crusoe' to all who loved him, and there was none who didn't. How he would have reacted to the solemn cricket of today will never be known; doubtless he would have caused much perturbation in Union circles. After watching an odd day's play at Brisbane in 1950–1 – England declared at 68 for 7, Australia at 32 for 7, whereupon England batted again and collapsed – he wrote that he had just witnessed 'The Marx Brothers at the Test'.

The essence of 'Crusoe' was that he found cricket funny – when he played (and he was a very fine fast-medium bowler) and when he wrote. But it was fun blended with kindness and admiration – witness his:

'After a short, galumphing run, like some policeman easing his conscience by a token pursuit of the uncatchable, Tate hurled into his delivery the harmonized strength of loins, back and fingers; a perfect engine.'

To read 'Crusoe' is to ask, 'How dare anyone else *try* to write about cricket?' Proof is required? The subject, Philip Mead of Hampshire and England:

'He was No. 4. Perhaps 2 wickets had fallen cheaply; and there the cheapness would end. He emerged from the pavilion with a strong, rolling gait; like a longshoreman with a purpose. He pervaded a cricket pitch. He occupied it and encamped on it. He erected a tent with a system of infallible pegging, then posted inexorable sentries. He took guard with the air of a guest who, having been offered a week-end by his host, obstinately decides to reside for six months. Having settled his whereabouts with the umpire, he wiggled the toe of his left boot for some fifteen seconds inside the crease, pulled the peak of a cap that seemed all peak, wiggled again, pulled again, then gave a comprehensive stare around him, as if to satisfy himself that no fielder, aware of the task ahead, had brought out a stick of dynamite. Then he leaned forward and looked at you down the pitch, quite still. His bat looked almost laughably broad.'

That was 'Crusoe'. Bless him!

30

It Won't Happen Again-3

When informed by the Somerset County Cricket Club that 1953 would be his Benefit year, the much respected all-rounder Bertie Buse chose the Lancashire game at Bath. This was a natural thing to do, Bath being Buse's home. On the other hand, it was not a sensible thing to do, the Recreation Ground wicket being somewhat eccentric. The previous summer a Middlesex batsman had, in the course of two deliveries from the slow left-arm Horace Hazell, been struck once on the toe and once in the eye.

On 6 June 1953 Buse and the Lancashire captain, Cyril Washbrook, inspected the pitch. 'Unfit for cricket,' opined Washbrook. But as the occasion was a special one, the game commenced. It seemed unlikely the wicket could deteriorate. Brian Statham bowled the first ball to Harold Gimblett who played forward. The ball shot upwards as on a whale-spout. Gimblett hit the spot where the ball had landed, and very soon was lost to view in a dust storm.

Washbrook bowled the off-spinner to Tattersall at the other end. His first delivery turned two feet and cleared the batsman's head. Somerset were out for 55 just after one o'clock. Each batsman had survived, on average, 15 deliveries. A venerable spectator mentioned that in 1905 he had watched the Australians play at Bath – Warwick Armstrong 303 not out. The observation seemed irrelevant.

Lancashire did better than Somerset, each of their batsmen averaging 19 deliveries at the crease. Their 150 owed much to Peter Marner and Alan Wharton who shared in a sixth-wicket partnership of 70 in 25 minutes. Marner's technique was

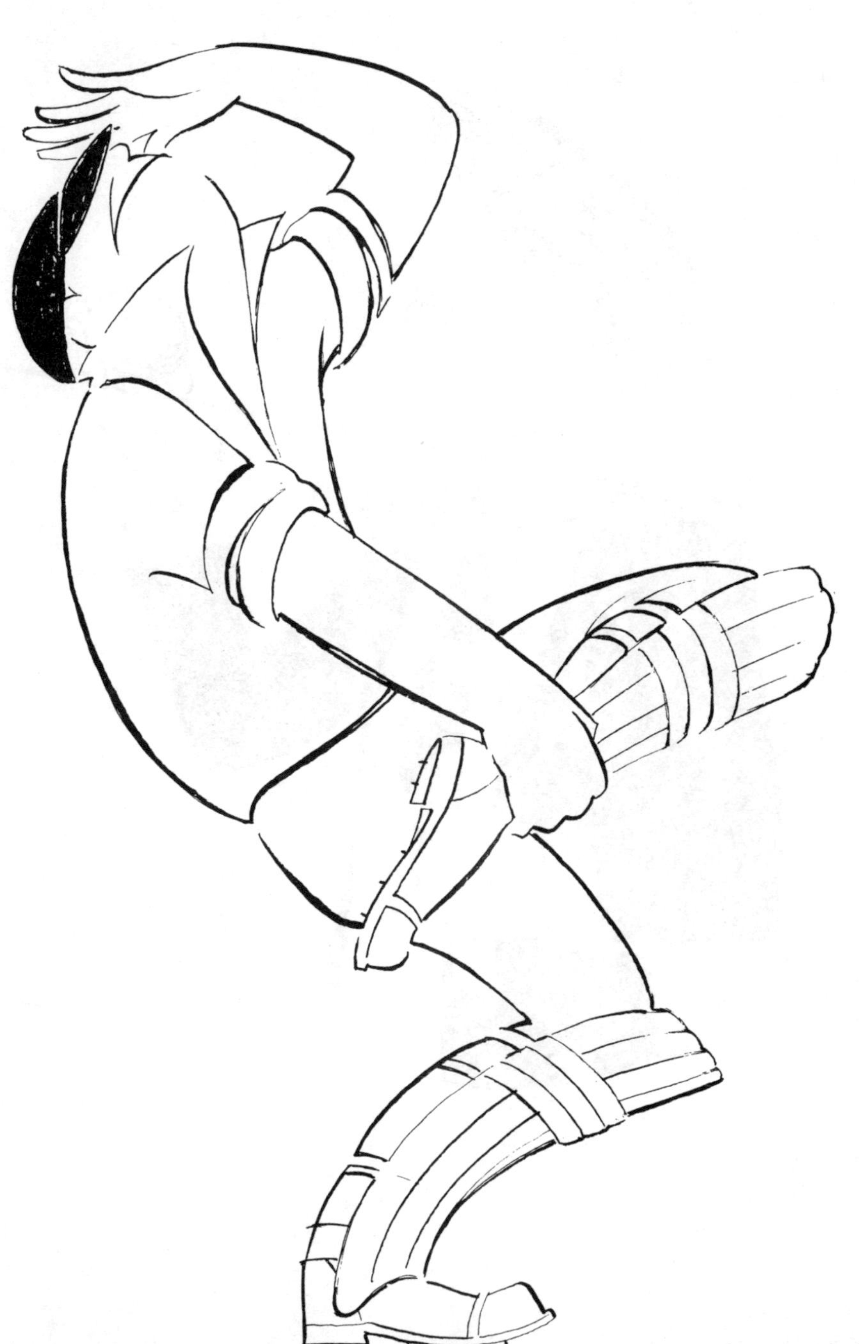

unusual but effective: he charged out to each ball and smote it hard and high.

During the interval before Somerset went in again, the County committee took umbrage and went into secret session. They resented a comment made in mid-afternoon that Her Majesty would refuse to allow the Royal horses to exercise on the Bath wicket for fear they damage a fetlock or two. The Somerset committee informed the press that cricketers do not have fetlocks.

Somerset's second innings lasted 13 balls fewer than their first. As Tattersall bowled his normal perfect length, he had match figures of 13 for 69. None of the batsmen raised much of a sweat. But members of the press were exhausted. During the day a wicket fell every 8 minutes 23 seconds. In late morning one pressman informed his paper that he was about to seek a lavatory. Running the two hundred yards, he returned to be told he had missed 1 run scored and 2 wickets fallen. After tea another pressman dashed off to buy a cup of tea and a doughnut. He missed no runs and 3 wickets. Before comparisons are made, it should be mentioned that the first pressman found the lavatory locked and had to climb in, while the second had to borrow a hammer to crack his doughnut.

The game ended soon after 5.30. Asked if he would like another Benefit, Bertie Buse said he couldn't afford one. The Somerset committee peered long at the cause of the trouble. They then held a press conference:

'We have no means of knowing how the wicket would have played on the second and third days of the match.'

Something like the above will never happen again at Bath. By the mid-sixties the Recreation Ground square was almost completely composed of cocksfoot and rye grass. The authorities at Taunton despatched a bucket of worms to Bath. Whether the worms would have improved the square was never clear, for they were eaten by crows. By 1966 children were picking dandelions and daisies from a good length.

Since then the pitch has played better. It is now cut and rolled.

31

Refreshments

When compiling a vast score at Canterbury, W. G. Grace once walked off the field and entered a tent where he knocked back a pint of champagne and seltzer. The fielders, of course, lay prostrate on the ground and waited for the Champion to return. This he did, considerably refreshed. In the 1880s and afterwards, before tea intervals were heard of, the great Arthur Shrewsbury of Nottinghamshire would seek out the dressing-room attendant after lunch and say, 'A cup of tea at four o'clock, please.' On the hour Shrewsbury received his cup, quaffed the contents, and went on batting.

In 1954, after many years watching the New York Yankees and others playing glorified rounders, Alistair Cooke returned to Old Trafford to watch a Test match. The tempo of play during the morning session was deliberate, neither batsmen nor bowlers suggesting animation. But at 1.30 all came to life and marched smartly off. Cooke raised an eyebrow. 'Lunch,' he was informed. At 4.15, after another session as deliberate as the first, the players again came to life and marched smartly off. Cooke raised his other eyebrow. 'Tea,' was the explanation.

The message had got through. When the players left the field at 6.30, Cooke beamed at his companion: 'I know – tomato-juice cocktails.'

During the twenties the American comedian Will Rogers once attended a cricket match where he was introduced to the then Prince of Wales, later King Edward VIII.

'Well, Mr Rogers, can you suggest any improvements to enliven this game?'

'Your Highness, if I was in charge I'd line up all the players before the game and say, "Now listen, fellers, no food till you're through."'

Whether Will Rogers would have applied this rule to the Durban Test in 1939, when South Africa and England played for ten days and then drew the match, is not known.

32

Laker and the Odds

Betting men may consider the odds.

To mid-July 1956 England and Australia had played one another 171 times.

In those 171 Tests an innings had been completed (i.e. 10 wickets had fallen) on 472 occasions.

Not once in those 472 innings had a bowler taken all 10 wickets.

At Old Trafford in 1956 Jim Laker became the first bowler to take all 10 wickets in a Test match innings. After Australia had followed on, five Englishmen bowled: Brian Statham 16 overs, Trevor Bailey 20, Laker 51.2, Tony Lock 55, and Alan Oakman 8. That is to say, four men bowled 594 balls and did not take a wicket; Laker bowled 308 balls and took 10 wickets.

What were the odds against this happening?

Laker's unlikely feat was rendered the more remarkable for two reasons:

Whether in first-class or in club cricket, the longer an innings lasts the less likely it is that one man will take all 10 wickets (there is always the likelihood of a run out, for instance). During the present century no fewer than 39 bowlers had taken all 10 wickets in a first-class innings, requiring on average 156 balls. But at Old Trafford Laker required 308, thus prompting the question 'What was happening at the other end?' Ironically, the other end was occupied by Lock, by far the most lethal spinner on turning pitches in England during the fifties.

Laker was an off-spinner, Lock a left-hander; Laker turned into a right-handed batsman, Lock turned away. Cricket lore insisted that a ball turning away from the batsman was the harder to play. In which case, why did Laker take 10 wickets and Lock none? Nine of Australia's batsmen were right-handers – the left-handers, Neil Harvey and Ken Mackay, both made 0, so that right-handers were baffled and bewildered by the ball coming into them.

Betting men will now re-consider the odds against Laker taking all 10 wickets, bearing in mind that Lock should have been the more dangerous bowler.

The Australian party of 1956 brought a full hand of fast or fast-medium bowlers – Ray Lindwall, Keith Miller, Alan Davidson, Ron Archer and Pat Crawford, Richie Benaud as wrist spinner, Ian Johnson (off-breaks) and Jack Wilson (left-arm) as finger spinners. Only one Test, at Lord's, favoured the seam, and Australia won – 5 wickets in each innings to Miller. The rest of the summer was Laker. Lock did not play in the Lord's match; in the other four, he took 15 wickets at 22.46 runs each to Laker's 43 at 8.79.

The Old Trafford Test saw England out 10 minutes after lunch on the second day for 459, Johnson and Benaud between them collecting 6 wickets for 274 from 94 overs. The runs suggested the wrong bowlers for the task in hand. As the wicket was brushed, dust arose. Colin McDonald and Jimmy Burke opened to the bowling of Statham and Bailey. Three overs from the latter, and Laker appeared; after 6 overs by Statham, Lock. It was all as decorous as a vicarage tea party. Seventeen overs from Laker and Lock produced nothing. Forty-eight for none.

3.55. Peter May switched his bowlers round. At once McDonald played forward and turned Laker to backward short-leg. Harvey went back to his third ball and was bowled. Sixty-two for 2 at tea, Burke and Craig in possession.

4.35. The vicarage tea party now resolved itself into a bun fight, the Englishmen grabbing all the food. Lock's first delivery lifted to Burke's glove, at slip Cowdrey swooped. Laker's first ball persuaded Craig to play back (from now there is no need to mention the bowler). Mackay prodded a catch to second slip. Miller drove Lock for 6, then was caught at short-leg. Benaud holed out at long-on. Archer charged down the pitch and missed; wicketkeeper Evans didn't. Maddocks and Johnson both went back to balls of good length.

5.15. Australia out for 84. Since tea Laker had taken 7 wickets for 8 runs from 22 *deliveries.*

5.25. McDonald and Burke took guard against Statham and Bailey. No trouble for the batsmen.

5.45. Laker again called up, before long joined by Lock. McDonald went off for treatment to an injured knee. Harvey entered and hit his first ball straight at Cowdrey at short and wide mid-on. Australia 53 for 1 at the close, Burke and Craig batting steadily.

Two days later Australia had advanced to 82 for 2 (Burke caught at leg-slip), the rains of Manchester dominant. On the fifth day play began only 10 minutes late; the pitch was dead, the sun did not come out until one o'clock, and Australia were 110 for 2 at lunch. After the interval, 4 wickets fell for 18 runs before Benaud joined McDonald. They lasted the 80 minutes until tea, taken with Australia 181 for 6.

The pitch meanwhile responded when the sun emerged, and eased when the sun went in. Craig batted for more than four hours, McDonald for five and a half hours, Benaud for over 100 minutes. The wicket was never sticky but a turner; Laker very rarely popped. The Australians succumbed only because Laker was relentlessly accurate, varying flight and spin. He was helped to all 10 wickets by Lock's unwillingness to pitch consistently on a good length. Wilfred Rhodes might have been driven on such a wicket; he would not, as Lock often was, have been pulled.

Laker's feat of all 10 wickets is likely to remain for all time in splendid isolation. We have moved into an age of seam or fast bowling. It is unlikely, to say the least, that some great West Indian fast bowler will emulate Laker; he will have three other fast bowlers to attack when he tires, and three bowlers are more likely to insist on a share of the spoils than one.

In the three-quarters of a century before Laker's 10 wickets in an innings, 427 Test matches were played. In little more than a quarter of a century since Laker at Old Trafford in 1956, that number has been exceeded! There is still only one bowler with all 10 wickets in an innings.

ENGLAND *v* AUSTRALIA

Old Trafford. 26, 27, 28, 30, 31 July 1956

England 459 (P. E. Richardson 104, M. C. Cowdrey 80, Rev. D. S. Sheppard 113)

AUSTRALIA

C. C. McDonald	c Lock b Laker	32	c Oakman b Laker	89
J. W. Burke	c Cowdrey b Lock	22	c Lock b Laker	33
R. N. Harvey	b Laker	0	c Cowdrey b Laker	0
I. D. Craig	lbw b Laker	8	lbw b Laker	38
K. R. Miller	c Oakman b Laker	6	b Laker	0
K. D. Mackay	c Oakman b Laker	0	c Oakman b Laker	0
R. G. Archer	st Evans b Laker	6	c Oakman b Laker	0
R. Benaud	c Statham b Laker	0	b Laker	18
R. R. Lindwall	not out	6	c Lock b Laker	8
L. Maddocks	b Laker	4	lbw b Laker	2
I. W. Johnson	b Laker	0	not out	1
Extras			B 12, LB 4	16
Total		84		205

Fall of wickets: 1–48, 2–48, 3–62, 4–62, 5–62, 6–73, 7–73, 8–78, 9–84, 10–84

Second innings: 1–28, 2–55, 3–114, 4–124, 5–130, 6–130, 7–181, 8–198, 9–203, 10–205

England Bowling

	O	M	R	W	O	M	R	W
Statham	6	3	6	0	16	10	15	0
Bailey	4	3	4	0	20	8	31	0
Laker	16.4	4	37	9	51.2	23	53	10
Lock	14	3	37	1	55	30	69	0
Oakman					8	3	21	0

ENGLAND WON BY AN INNINGS AND 170 RUNS

33

Happy Warriors

Let's choose a team of lovely men. Because somewhere, at this very moment, cricketers are fighting, scratching, snorting, arguing, refusing to play, agreeing to play only if they can first have special corn flakes for breakfast, hitting umpires, kicking over stumps – doing everything to make a great game resemble a meeting of politicians. Come to think of it, cricketers are getting worse than politicians.

Our team of lovely men must not consist of mediocrities who, lacking ability, play the fool. Far from it – our lovely men will be at least magnificent, in many instances great cricketers. They will give pleasure not only for their skills but also for their approach to the game. They need not be eccentric like George Gunn who, not content with wandering down the wicket to fast bowlers, once enraged Learie Constantine by putting his tongue out whenever a bumper threatened him. Besides, if the weather was too hot for George, he would flick 20 or so in half an hour, then deliberately get out and spend the rest of the day in a deck-chair, or shopping with his wife.

For tactical reasons we shall omit the obvious first choice among happy warriors – Jack Hobbs. Whatever the state of the pitch, the opposition would have small chance of dismissing him if he was trying, and would therefore vent the venom of their spleen on his team mates. It will be noted that the opposition consists of (and we must be tactful) unlovely warriors fully determined to win by means fair or foul. Which is a reminder that umpires are important. Without hesitation we insist on Frank Chester at his pre-war peak, and Syd Buller. Any nonsense from the opposition . . .

The greatest of all bowlers, S. F. Barnes, does not qualify for our team of happy warriors; in fact, he will be No. 1 among the awkward cusses. With a little luck, Barnes will have several catches missed off his bowling; smoke rising, he will explode – to be met with a peremptory, 'Shut up, Syd, and get on with it' from umpire Chester-Buller. This will prevent Barnes from walking from the field in high dudgeon. Frank Chester once had an appeal for lbw directed at him by Hedley Verity who was most abstemious in his demands. 'Not out. That was a bad

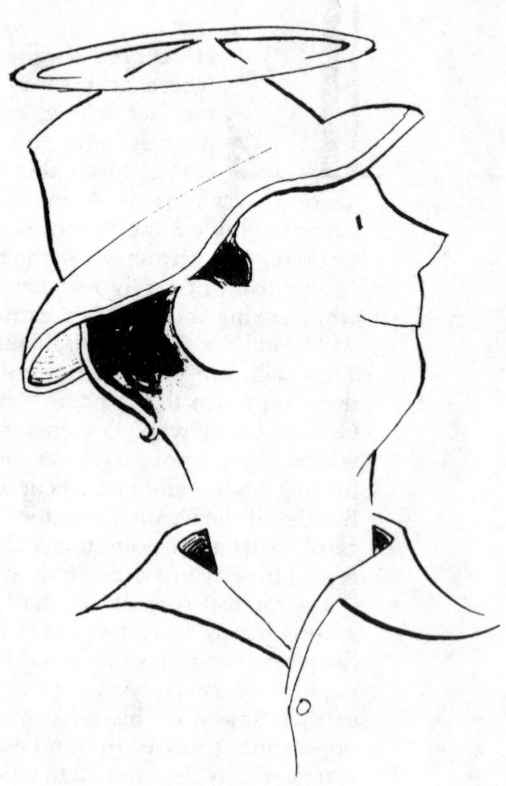

appeal, Hedley – and you know it!' Verity, being Verity, smiled and went on bowling.

The fact that Barnes will bowl against our happy warriors presents us with a problem: does the South African Herbie Taylor qualify? In 1913–14, as one of by far the weaker side, he faced Barnes on the mat and scored 109, 8, 29, 40, 14, 70, 16 and 93 (42 and 87 in the fifth Test when Barnes was absent) in addition to a century for Natal in the only game lost by

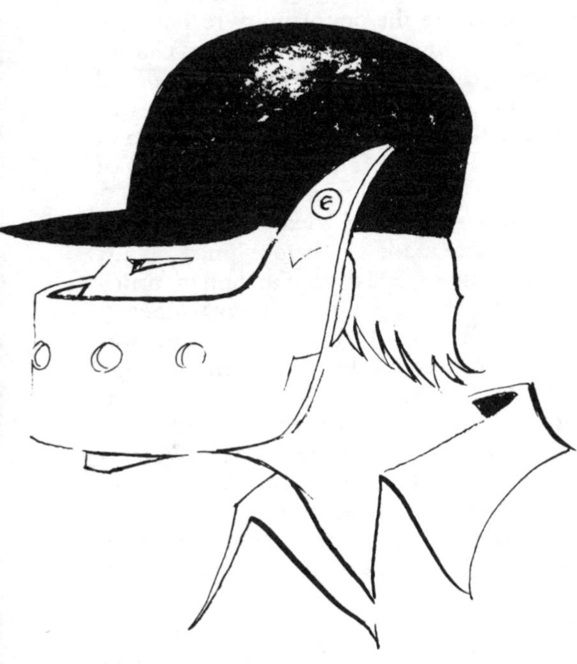

MCC. It was then that Taylor so frustrated Barnes that the bowler threw down the ball and stalked off the field – at least that was Taylor's story, and it sounds a likely one. However, though Taylor was a great batsman and theorist, perhaps he lacked a sense of humour; after the 'Battle of Adelaide' in 1933, a pressman asked him what he thought of bodyline. 'There is no danger if the batsmen play forward.'

So unless Barnes is seen approaching the ground with a roll of matting under his arm (not that he *needed* matting to bowl on!) we shall opt for Roy McLean, a Cavalier batsman if ever there was one, and a delightful personality withal. He brought light to South African cricket in what was sometimes a dour period. He will also appreciate the opportunity to bat with Prince Duleepsinhji, a stroke player of genius and most charming of men. Many insist that had not ill-health compelled Duleep to retire from first-class cricket long before he was thirty, the decade before the Second World War in England might have been known as The Age of Duleep – and not that of Hammond.

Our opening pair are indisputably Victor Trumper and Colin Milburn. Trumper once made 100 before lunch against England; bowlers found it impossible to contain him in form – 'Spoil a bowler's length and you've got him.' Sunny tempered, he was (in Plum Warner's words) 'as modest as he was magnificent'. As partner the massively built Milburn – a happy warrior even after losing the sight of his left eye in a car accident aged twenty-seven – will enjoy waiting upon Trumper. Perhaps 'waiting upon' is inaccurate; playing for Western Australia against Queensland, Milburn once made 181 in the two hours between lunch and tea. A superb hooker, and able to drive through the covers with the power of Hammond, Milburn will complement Trumper's effortless style. Lunch score 200 for none . . .

On the other hand, Trumper did have a fondness for playing back cuts at the swinging new ball, and Milburn would consider it no disgrace to be caught on the boundary after striking 50 in an hour. In short, something may go wrong with our openers. So No. 3 must be Lindsay Hassett, a great batsman though five foot six who, in the first two Australian series *v* England after 1939–45, had the unenviable task of going in No. 4 *after Bradman*. In his youth before the war, he was brilliant, not beyond dancing out to O'Reilly and hitting him over the pickets. 'And you're not even good-looking,' responded the Tiger on one occasion. Poker-faced Hassett is our captain; the opposition will be prepared for wit, most subtly concealed. At Oxford in 1948 the University captain asked Lindsay what roller he'd like on – 'Heavy? Light?' Without a flicker came the query, 'Haven't you a spiked one?'

And should things go very wrong with our happy warriors, the most consoling of sights will be Maurice Leyland. Broad-bottomed and with forearms like Yorkshire hams, Maurice did not know the meaning of 'lost cause'. Humour exuded from this Tyke; when Walter Robins joined him in the England second innings at Melbourne in 1936–7 – half their wickets gone and needing close on 500 to win, Leyland was compelled to take some short singles. 'Steady laad! Can't get all ruddy roons t'neet!' Maurice also purveyed the chinaman form of left-arm attack, sometimes omitting to hit the deck. At Sheffield in 1940, Bradman made 140 in a couple of hours. And how was he out? According to the bowler, 'T'Don were tired out, bowled Leyland.'

Our wicketkeeper may have to be press-ganged, but we intend to have New Zealand's most comprehensive cricketer, John Reid. Was he a happy warrior? He was. Did he once keep wicket for his country at the Oval? He did. Did he once tour South Africa, scoring over 1,000 runs and taking 50 wickets? Did he once hit fifteen 6s in a first-class innings, a little matter of 296? The answer to most questions about John Reid on the cricket field is Yes. Should he become bored behind the stumps, Lindsay Hassett will relieve him for a few overs.

So far seven happy batsmen, only one of whom (with Reid keeping wicket) bowls a bit. Here we insist that the side first appears on a pre-war Headingley strip with those two high priests of Yorkshire efficiency, Wilfred Rhodes and Emmott Robinson, obliged to watch Leyland dispensing eccentricities. 'Dost see what our Maurice is up to?' 'Ay! Not foony.' To placate the high priests we must choose a couple of great opening bowlers.

Only one of them shall be fast. The appeal of cricket is one of contrasts; perfection can grow tedious. If every bowler above medium-pace – whether Test class or merely village green – had an action resembling that of Larwood or Lindwall, Lillee or Holding, we should cease to appreciate them. The glorious action is emphasized by the surrounding carthorses; if every town boasted a Placido Domingo, who would bother to hear the great man himself? We shall choose a great fast bowler and a great medium-pace bowler.

Acknowledging that with the exception (and what an exception!) of Duleepsinhji, our side is not going to be strong in slip fielders, we go for a fast bowler who just shakes his head sadly when a sitter is missed. He will bowl at the stumps with relentless accuracy, preferring to root-up wood rather than dent a batsman's head. Brian Statham is our man. At the other end who else than the incomparable giant, long time adversary and friend of Hassett, and striving as hard during the closing overs as at the start of play – Alec Bedser?

All bowlers are happy when they take wickets; that wonderful Australian Bill Johnston was happy just to be in flannels. At fast-medium left-arm over the wicket, he could cause as much consternation as Lindwall and Miller; when the pitch began to crumble, Johnston reduced his pace and spun the ball beautifully. The bucking and plunging approach (John Arlott's phrase) was also carried over into Johnston's batting – at least it was on one occasion. Johnston a batsman? Certainly. Thanks in part to Lindsay Hassett's foresight, he was one of two touring batsmen to average over 100 during a tour of England. (Does some reader really say he can't guess the identity of the other?)

When Johnston went out to bat at Scarborough in the last game of the 1953 tour, he took with him a note from Hassett to the opposing captain, Norman Yardley – 'Dear Norman, Please look after Bill. Lindsay.' The No. 10 then got himself out before Bill could receive a ball, leaving him bashfully smiling at four months' success:

Inns 17, TNO 16, Runs 102, HS 28 not out, Av. 102.00

And there will certainly be no need to tell Hassett that one of his batsmen must feign injury so that Bill Johnston may run for him. He did this for Ernie Toshack at Headingley in 1948, the effect being that of some Keystone Kop after drinking elderberry wine.

Finally, the happiest of all happy warriors – Arthur Mailey. His first over will consist of a full-toss, a polyhop (naturally both hit for 4), a couple of leg-breaks pitching outside the leg stump and missing the off, another full-toss and finally a googly which breaks a couple of feet and takes the leg bail. All members of the press will explain at length how they would play such rubbish, Mailey replying with some of his delectable caricatures.

Anything lacking? Yes, a manager to make after-dinner speeches of such charm and wit that any politician present will slink from the room ashamed of his breed. Prevailed upon to show his skills, the manager will remove his jacket and send down some lethal deliveries with a bread roll. The cross-talk act between manager and captain Hassett will convulse; should trouble threaten, the manager will send for his friend the Lord Chancellor. Our manager will be – must be – Sir Learie Nicholas Constantine, Lord Constantine of Nelson and every ground where he played cricket.

We are proud of our team, and so spectators too.

Victor Trumper
Colin Milburn
Lindsay Hassett
Prince Duleepsinhji
Roy McLean
Maurice Leyland
John Reid
Alec Bedser
Brian Statham
Bill Johnston
Arthur Mailey

And will this team win? Win! They probably will; if they don't, they will still be happy warriors.

The opposition, consisting of awkward cusses, bloody-minded tyrants, unpleasant sods and the like? The reader has a pencil and paper.

34

Judgement

From time to time young cricketers will insist that if the giants of earlier years were playing today, they would find the modern game too difficult for them. Hobbs and Hammond, Bradman and McCabe, George Headley and Dudley Nourse must inevitably be baffled by 'scientific field placings' and the like. This implies that when Bradman faced O'Reilly in a Shield game, or Verity in a Test, the fielders wandered about as they liked.

Another point of view was expressed by Sir Leonard Hutton in 1978. His career for Yorkshire had spanned the years 1934–55; among the spin bowlers he had faced either in the middle or at the nets were Fleetwood-Smith and Verity, Laker and Lock, the Australians Iverson and Benaud, the West Indians Ramadhin and Valentine, the South Africans Rowan and Mann. All were considered pretty good in their day. But consider Hutton's judgement of 1978:

'Once, in my early days with Yorkshire, I saw Wilfred Rhodes in the dressing-room during a match at Sheffield. I asked him if he would come round to the nets and bowl a few at me. For twenty minutes Wilfred bowled in his braces. It was a revelation: never before *or since* (our italics) has a bowler made me misjudge the length of a ball as Rhodes did.'

We may note that when Hutton first played for Yorkshire in 1934, Rhodes was in his fifty-seventh year. Therefore it is not hard to understand why, in 1903–4 on a blazing day at Sydney, Victor Trumper – on his way to 185 not out – had smiled at the end of an over by Rhodes and said, 'Give me some peace, Wilf!'

After the Second World War Hutton arrived in Adelaide

with an MCC party. Waiting at the nets was a wizened little man who asked if he might bowl a few. Of course! So Clarrie Grimmett, aged fifty-four or so, put Hutton through his paces – and the batsmen wondered at the consummate cunning of the master.

Of course, we may argue that Hutton couldn't bat.

35

83 Per Cent

On 30 June 1977 Glenn Turner, Worcestershire's New Zealand batsman, played Glamorgan at Swansea. Opening the innings, he was responsible for 83 per cent of his side's runs – a world record.

WORCESTER – First Innings

			Fall of Wkt.
G. M. Turner	not out	141	
B. J. R. Jones	lbw, b Nash	1	1– 18
P. A. Neale	c E. Jones, b Wilkins	3	2– 35
J. Cumbes	lbw, b Nash	5	3– 68
E. J. O. Hemsley	b Cordle	3	4– 71
B. L. D'Oliveira	c E. Jones, b Cordle	0	5– 71
D. J. Patel	c E. Jones, b Nash	4	6– 82
D. J. Humphries	c Llewellyn, b Cordle	0	7– 87
V. A. Holder	lbw, b Cordle	4	8– 93
N. G. Gifford	c Lllewellyn, b Lloyd	7	9–150
A. P. Pridgeon	lbw, b Cordle	0	10–169
Extras (lb 1)		1	
Total		169	

GLAMORGAN BOWLING

	O.	M.	R.	W.
M. A. Nash	31	14	51	3
A. R. Cordle	24	10	53	5
A. H. Wilkins	7	0	33	1
R. C. Ontong	3	0	20	0
B. J. Lloyd	3	1	11	1

The highest individual scores to constitute a high percentage of an innings were 385 out of 500 (77 per cent) by Bert Sutcliffe, Otago *v* Canterbury 1952–3; and Vijay Hazare's 309 out of 387 (79 per cent), Rest *v* Hindus 1943–4.

36

Salute to Supermen

It's good to talk of great men, better still to recall great teams. 'Recall' – that's the operative word. From what age does a person have a fairly critical memory of what he saw? It varies; all one can say with assurance is that a critical memory entails comparisons. A ten-year-old boy living in Little Tiddlebury and watching the local cricketers week by week, could be taken to see Hammond or Larwood, Zaheer or Holding, and realize at once they were wonderful.

But he wouldn't know *why* until he saw them playing with their Test colleagues. He couldn't begin to criticize them unless able to compare. Shall we suggest that fifteen may be the age when the average boy begins to criticize and compare *instinctively*? It may be earlier, or later. If we are approximately right in suggesting fifteen, then we realize at once the difficulty in judging great sides.

Joe Darling's 1902 Australians were acclaimed as great. But the fifteen-year-old who saw them is now almost certainly dead. Warwick Armstrong's 1921 Australians trampled over English cricket; many in their middle-seventies will remember them, but not nearly as many as would have ten years ago. It's not really possible to compare crickets or teams fifty years or more apart.

So let's talk about great teams since the Second World War. The fifteen-year-old who watched cricket in 1948 has not yet reached his fiftieth birthday. He may look old to today's schoolboys but not venerable. Damn it! He can still bend, get his arm over, see the scoreboard . . . Yes, great teams since 1945 who've toured England.

John Goddard's West Indians of 1950 were indeed superb,

so far as they went. Considering they beat England 3–1, that 'so far as they went' may sound odd. They had a very fine opening pair in Jeffrey Stollmeyer and Rae, and then came the tremendous trio of Worrell, Weekes and Walcott. Three truly great batsmen one after the other: Frank Worrell, who afforded the same sort of pleasure Barry Richards would years later; Everton Weekes, a Bradman-esque butcher; and Clyde Walcott, a giant to whom the bravest cover-point retreated some yards. And there was more batting to come.

But what if 1950 had not been the summer of Denis Compton's knee operation? Could he have got after Sonny Ramadhin – as Keith Miller and other Australians would in due course – and knocked him out of the firing line? We shall never know. Ramadhin bowled off-breaks and leg-breaks, bemusing England most horribly; at the other end Alfred Valentine's classic left-arm spin proved just as troublesome. The two spinners *were* West Indies' attack; had they been collared, anything might have happened. For this was the only Test side from the Caribbean not to include a great, or potentially great, fast bowler. For that reason we conclude that the 1950 West Indies side was superb in parts but not a unit for all occasions.

Thirteen years later there was but a single flaw in Worrell's team. Conrad Hunte, an opening batsman of the highest class, had no worthy partner; three men were tried, and in 9 innings they combined to average 14. A great Test team must have a great pair of openers. For the rest all was memorable. The bowling perplexed batsmen and pleased the eye. It is often argued that a Test team requires as much bowling as it can lay hands on; this is sheer nonsense so long as the specialist bowlers are outstanding. Look for a moment at the past.

The 1921 Australians conquered with four bowlers: Gregory and Macdonald fast, Armstrong a master of length, and Mailey with leg-breaks and googlies. The observant reader will here cry 'Foul!' and point out that Gregory and Armstrong were all-rounders. Of course! But they were also specialist bowlers. Think of the effect had the following been contemporaneous and born in the same country: Keith Miller and Sobers to open, with Armstrong, M. A. Noble's off-breaks, and the South African Aubrey Faulkner's leg-breaks. All specialist batsmen, all specialist bowlers – with Sobers able to bowl in three different styles.

Worrell's 1963 West Indian attack was four-pronged: Wesley Hall and Charlie Griffith both very fast, Gibbs's off-breaks, and Sobers. Four men: six bowlers! Between them they accounted for 95 per cent of their side's overs, and 96 per cent of the wickets – Worrell lending a paternal hand when necessary with a few overs. The perfectly balanced bowling attack. No leg-spinner; otherwise comprehensive in scope. To score enough runs for these men to bowl against, there was Hunte, the exotic Rohan Kanhai (his tour-de-force a sweep which sent the ball into the crowd, and left the striker on his back!); Basil Butcher, Joe Solomon, Worrell – and Sobers. With an opening partner for Hunte, surely one of the half-dozen finest of teams. It defeated England three matches to one.

Can Worrell's side be trumped? Before middle-aged men mutter the magic date '1948', we must note one of cricket's little ironies – that in 1948 England's batting started with Hutton, Washbrook, Bill Edrich and Compton, with only Alec Bedser as a consistently effective bowler, whereas in 1963 England's bowling (Trueman, Statham, Shackleton, Lock, and the off-spinners Titmus and David Allen) restricted West Indies to few more than 300 runs an innings, only to see the batting humbled by Hall, Griffith and company. The England batting of 1948, with the England bowling of 1963, would have given West Indies an almighty tussle.

1948–1963; Bradman's Australians – Worrell's West Indians. Both captains were in their cricketing dotage, both displayed tactical expertise amounting to second sight; in terms of leadership neither put a foot wrong. But whereas Bradman still occupied the No. 3 position, Worrell was content to direct operations from No. 6 or 7. As batsman, therefore, Bradman was the more important. But, in judging the two sides man for man, should we compare Bradman with the West Indian captain or with the No. 3, Kanhai? While readers debate this point, let's jot down the teams as they appeared at their strongest, remembering that a new ball was available every 55 overs in 1948 but every 85 overs in 1963. This law naturally affected bowling tactics, the 'holding' operation until the opening pair were brought back into action being much briefer in 1948.

AUSTRALIA: S. G. Barnes, A. R. Morris, D. G. Bradman, A. L. Hassett, K. R. Miller, R. N. Harvey, D. Tallon (wicket-keeper), I. W. Johnson, R. R. Lindwall, W. A. Johnston, E. R. H. Toshack.

WEST INDIES: C. C. Hunte, E. D. McMorris or M. C. Carew, R. B. Kanhai, B. F. Butcher, G. S. Sobers, J. S. Solomon, F. M. Worrell, D. L. Murray (wicketkeeper), W. W. Hall, C. C. Griffith, L. R. Gibbs.

Bearing in mind that Australia's batsmen had an easier task in 1948, and their bowlers a more difficult one (see above) we must first note the composite balance of the teams. The top six Australians could all rank as specialist batsmen, the top seven West Indians. But whereas Australia had, in effect, three all-rounders (Miller, Tallon and Lindwall), West Indies had only one (Sobers) – or, if we include Worrell, one and a bit. To add to our confusion, we must explain the presence of Toshack in the Australian side. Bowling left-arm over the wicket at more medium than slow in pace, he put a break in England's scoring until the new ball should be available after 55 overs.

How do we equate the specialist bowlers? For Australia Lindwall and Miller opened, for West Indies Hall and Griffith. The off-spinners were Ian Johnson and Gibbs, the left-arm medium-pacers Toshack and Worrell. Which brings us to two key men, both left-arm and both capable of bowling in more than one style – Bill Johnston and Sobers. Of Sobers the all-rounder nothing more needs to be said; of Johnston, either at fast-medium or in his very plausible imitation of Verity, only that he was in many ways the lynch pin of Bradman's attack. When either Lindwall or Miller was unable to bowl through injury, Johnston took over; when the pitch began to take spin, Johnston was the key man. Without him, Bradman must needs have played one of his leg-spinners, McCool or Ring – neither in the Grimmett-O'Reilly class.

Faced then with much dissimilarity, with the fact that Griffith's faster ball was regarded by many as somewhat suspect (as English umpires did not call him, this point must be ignored) with an obligation to judge men on performance and not on reputation – above all by the contrasting English strengths of 1948 and 1963, we may risk judging the players thus. A + indicates superiority, = of equal effect.

AUSTRALIA 1948	WEST INDIES 1963
= Barnes	= Hunte
+ Morris	McMorris/Carew
= Bradman	= Kanhai
= Hassett	= Butcher
+ Harvey	Solomon
Miller (as batsman)	+ Sobers (as batsman)
= Miller (as bowler)	= Griffith
+ Johnston	Sobers (as bowler)
+ Lindwall	Hall
+ Tallon	Murray
Johnson	+ Gibbs
= Toshack (as bowler)	= Worrell (as batsman)

Some will argue that Murray, who did nothing wrong in the Tests of 1963, was therefore the equal of Tallon. So be it.

How did the sides compare as a whole? West Indies lost one Test and won three, Australia won four; West Indies also lost to Yorkshire. Bradman's Australians went through 1948 unbeaten. To show the relative strengths and weaknesses of England in the two summers – and these figures assume that 110 overs were bowled daily, as in 1948:

BATTING *v* ENGLAND

AUSTRALIA 1948		WEST INDIES 1963
480	Av. Total/compl. inns.	312
9 hrs. 20 mins	Scored in	6 hrs. 45 mins

BOWLING *v* ENGLAND

ENGLAND 1948		ENGLAND 1963
291	Av. Total/compl. inns.	247
6 hrs. 45 mins	Scored in	5 hrs. 10 mins

Let the argument begin! Incidentally, soon after the Australians of 1948 and the West Indians of 1963 returned home, knighthoods were conferred on Donald George Bradman and Frank Maglinne Worrell.

37

Why Five-Day Tests?

In 1930 Bobby Jones won the Open played over 72 holes, Bill Tilden won the Men's Singles at Wimbledon – the best of five sets; the summer's Tests between England and Australia were each limited to four days, with the proviso the last would be played to a finish if the sides were level. Today the Open is still of 72 holes, men at Wimbledon still play the best of five sets. Test matches sprawl over five days instead of four. Why?

But first let's consider the joke contained in the above. Prior to the Australian tour of 1930, *all* Tests in England had been of three days' duration (although the final game of 1926 had been played to a finish – in the event over on the fourth day). Indeed, until 1947 all Tests played in England, except for the Australian tours of the thirties, were allotted *three* days. Reminded of this, the pundits will say, 'Ah! but what is more boring than a cricket match destined from the start to be drawn?'

Consider then Tests played in England against Australia during the present century:

	Duration	*Percentage finished*
1902–26	3 days	48
1930–38	4 days	53
1948–81	5 days	52

Cricket's administrators have, in effect, commanded players to be dull. Sixty years ago the only difference between a County game and a Test match in England was that the latter had more outstanding cricketers on parade. But the tempo was basically the same.

It is the duty of cricketers (Test, County or Club) to adapt themselves to the time limit prescribed. Given ten days, a side's aim would be to bat for four days, score 600, and wear the pitch. But within the old three days' span of 19 hours (11.30–6.30 on the first day, 11–6.30 on the second and third), a side batting first sought to score – and often did – 350 on the first day. One result of this was that the side so scoring had made itself more or less immune from defeat.

Given a good wicket and two evenly balanced teams, a five-day Test can easily be drawn. Before Old Trafford 1964 Australia were one-up and had only to draw to retain the Ashes. Winning the toss, they made 658 for 8 declared, England replying with 611. Australia's second innings consisted of a single over!

'But that was an isolated instance,' says the reader, 'you couldn't have a whole series like that.'

In 1960–1 India and Pakistan played a series of five-day Tests. All were drawn. Each game averaged 932 runs for the loss of 24 wickets. Doubtless the spectators assured themselves they had been watching cricket. But spectators have been brain-washed into believing that anything labelled 'Test match' is automatically worth watching. They shall be reminded of Parkinson's Law:

'Work expands so as to fill the time available for its completion.' In cricket terms it may be interpreted thus: A three-day Test saw a total of 360 overs bowled. Therefore the daily number was $\frac{360}{3} = 120$. To find the number of overs bowled daily in a five-day Test, the problem becomes $\frac{360}{5} = 72$. Should any indignant bowler react angrily to this, he shall be reminded that during the 1976–7 series, India and England averaged 72 overs a day.

Of course the over-rate has declined. Only a fool expects an 800 metres runner to move at the same speed as a man engaged in a 100 metres sprint. Similarly with bowlers. Tell a man on Thursday morning that he will still be taking part in the same game on the following Tuesday evening, and he naturally paces himself accordingly. Meanwhile the administrators natter and seek to introduce penalties. The problem they have to solve concerns not the over-rate but the duration of Tests.

The two are linked, but a shortening of Test hours will surely raise the over-rate. Between the wars in England 43 Tests were played over three days, each day producing on average 340 runs. The first 43 Tests to be played after the Second World War *over five days* produced 274 runs a day –

THE OVER RATE IN BOTH PERIODS THE SAME. Gradually the over-rate fell.

At the end of an English season the first-class averages are based on the runs made, and the wickets taken, in games between the counties, between counties and the tourists and in Test matches. County cricket is first-class cricket, its games played over three days; Test cricket is also first-class cricket but its games may occupy five days. Why?

A quarter of a century ago, when he was England's greatest batsman, Peter May suggested that four days were ample for a Test. May is now Chairman of the England Selectors.

Afterword

IAN BOTHAM By Kenneth Gregory

Botham the cricketer is a throw-back to the Golden Age – those twenty years preceding the Great War. Everything he achieves (or does not achieve) can be seen in these terms. If his success in Test matches bewilders, that is only because we have grown accustomed to hours of grinding monotony from players persuaded it is necessary to lower their sights when wearing an England cap.

We live in an age of theory. If the ball does not come on to the bat, then it is impossible to play attacking strokes. Botham with a bat in his hands is no theorist: if the ball does not come on to the bat, then let the bat go to the ball. In short, hit the bloody thing. Here we should point out – for even in our television-dominated days there are people somewhere who have not seen Botham – that he is a big man of enormous strength. At worst, he can bash a ball and often get away with strokes which played by another man would be disastrous.

We live in an age of mealy-mouthedness. During the 1932–3 bodyline tour, Jack Fingleton had the misfortune to make a 'pair'. Remarking what a terrible thing it was to happen to a young man, R. G. Menzies asked Warwick Armstrong why he supposed it had come about. The Big Ship answered briefly: 'Can't bat!' A harsh and untrue judgement but preferable to the reactions of modern pundits who advanced theories of unplayable pitches, scientifically-placed fields and the like. When Botham fails with the bat, faces drop; then, 'Just wait till the second innings!' Spectators have faith in Botham because Botham has faith in himself.

He is, in essence, an amateur cricketer. He plays as amateurs used to play if they were good enough (the Golden Age, as we

shall see, was full of them). In the late forties E. W. Swanton was asked to name the batsman who personified the amateur approach: Denis Compton! That great man, we need hardly add, was paid to play cricket. So with Botham: he enjoys cricket, he conveys his sense of enjoyment to the crowd and, because he is good enough, he triumphs often against odds.

In one sense, Botham the batsman is the luckiest of contemporary players: he has a twin, Botham the bowler. Test selectors mope when Botham the batsman fails but they don't think of dropping him – Botham the bowler being England's most successful bowler. (Of Botham the slip fielder, we content ourselves with the observation that he performs like a plunging porpoise – not as noble as Hammond but often as effective.) And Botham is frequently England's most successful bowler because he is a throw-back to the Golden Age.

At a lively fast-medium pace, Botham bowls a prodigious out-swinger (he naturally swings the other way as well when working out a plan). Lots of bowlers are expert with out-swing but few attack to Botham's full length. He invites batsmen to play strokes on the off-side; a great batsman probably finds Botham easier to score off than he does other defensively-minded bowlers. He also finds him easier to get out to. In the Golden Age bowlers encouraged batsmen to play their off-side strokes (apologizing to captains if they let one go down the leg-side); batsmen complied, made runs and got out. Botham is an attacking bowler, hence the seemingly absurd number of times when he will take 5 wickets in an innings.

Botham the batsman came into Test cricket when the England side was suffering from Boycott-itis. The complaint may be described thus: noting that a certain opener of supreme application, concentration and (when he chose to play them) the possessor of all the strokes made large scores, other batsmen took the hint. Now while almost every team must include one Boycott (and it doesn't matter if his name is Herbert Sutcliffe, John Edrich or Bill Lawry) it is unbearable and pointless when a side includes one authentic Boycott and several second or third-rate Boycotts. The authentic Boycott proclaims himself, the pale imitations only inadequate methods.

A batsman must be true to himself; he must also be relevant to the situation in which he finds himself. Botham's good fortune was that he could be true to himself and (because he was good enough) so help England out of various predicaments. To Botham a bowler is a man whose task it is to wait upon Botham. This batsman's methods scorn diplomatic niceties and are intent on most fearful aggression. As we have seen, Botham salutes Lillee as a master of his craft, but that is no reason why Botham should not seek to hit him into the stands. Such a stroke will annoy Lillee; Botham the batsman likes to annoy bowlers.

If we are looking for a batsman to play for our lives, we shall pass Botham by; but if we are hiring a man to destroy an attack consisting of the world's best bowlers, we shall place our money on Botham of current England batsmen. In such circumstances no man can guarantee results – after all, Victor Trumper once had successive Test innings against England of 4, 0, 0, 0, 10 before shattering Barnes, Wilfred Rhodes, Jack Crawford and Braund to the tune of 166. Trumper was Prince of the Golden Age, Botham has fun as marauding Emperor of our own Age of Lead. An hour of Botham transmutes lead into 22-carat gold.

The records inform us that Botham was only just twenty-six when he reached his Test 'double' of 2,000 runs and 200 wickets. Ignore such records. They prove only that Botham was born at the right time – that by the occasion of his twenty-sixth birthday, or soon after, he had appeared in forty-two Tests without getting injured. At the same age, Keith Miller had played in only three Tests, Jack Gregory in ten – both careers affected by world wars. Wilfred Rhodes's early career was not affected by war, but by his twenty-sixth birthday he had played only eight times for England – Tests being few and far between. Botham's 2,000 runs and 200 wickets 'double' means little or nothing; what means everything is the Botham method.

It is pleasant for a cricketer to know that by the age of twenty-six he is immortal (we shall even tempt the gods and say that if Botham never scores another run, or takes another wicket in Tests, he is still immortal). Botham achieved this state of bliss by brandishing a fist, saying to himself, 'I, alone, can do it!' and rousing a nation. At the risk of embarrassing Botham, we shall suggest that he roused a nation by treating it to the cricketing equivalent of Churchillian oratory at a time when it had grown accustomed to hearing stockbrokers' reports read aloud. Botham may know he is good – it would be hypocrisy to suggest otherwise; but we doubt if he fully appreciates *why* in 1981 he was twice sublime.

Heroism in cricket, as in all walks of life, is encountered but rarely. At the Oval in 1902 Gilbert Jessop went in at 48 for 5, with England needing to score 263 in the last innings on a rain-damaged pitch. Jessop made a century in 75 minutes. At Melbourne in 1907–8 Kenneth Hutchings shattered an Australian attack consisting of 'Tibby' Cotter, Jack Saunders, Noble, Armstrong, Jerry Hazlitt and Macartney, his 126 studded with 25 boundaries. At Lord's in 1930 Percy Chapman almost saved England with a century defying belief, his favourite stroke a pull off Grimmett into the Mound Stand.

Greatest of all was Stanley McCabe's 187 not out at Sydney in 1932–3 off England's 'bodyline' attack which precluded him almost completely from scoring in front of the wicket on the off-side. (McCabe followed with 189 not out at Johannesburg in 1935–6 – much of it played in semi-darkness, and 232 at Trent Bridge in 1938 – much of it with three tail-enders at the other end.) It is the measure of Botham in 1981 that he merits to be spoken of in the same breath as McCabe.

The story will be told as long as cricket is played. How at Headingley England had followed on 227 behind, how shortly after Botham came in a second time they were 133 for 7, how the batsman then made an undefeated 145 in three and a half hours before the close on the fourth day. One 6 and twenty-six 4s were the mightiest of Botham's strokes. The why and the wherefore? Australia were playing a three-man attack – Lillee, Alderman and Lawson (Bright present but not used). Let us concede that a side which, for any reason you like, goes into a Test with three bowlers is asking for trouble; that Lillee, Alderman and Lawson must have lost something of their sting if not of their expertise by the time Botham arrived; that Dilley (56), Old (29) and Willis were not meant to stay long as Botham's partners. They did, while 221 runs were added.

In isolation, this innings proclaimed Botham as a superb destroyer able to ride his good fortune; in isolation, it was a magnificent freak of an innings. Botham, we felt, could never repeat it. He did not – or has not to date. But a month later at Old Trafford, he wrought a miracle of McCabe-like genius (we are choosing words parsimoniously and with care). Then, in her second innings, England had struggled to 104 off 70 overs, a balance suggesting stroke-making was impossible. At first Botham agreed with this diagnosis, scoring a mere 5 runs from 32 balls. 23 runs from 21 balls followed, and then . . .

The new ball! Whisper those dreaded words. Remark upon

the suspicion they cause to enter men's minds. Inside Botham's mind there must be some retarded specimen of a theorist capable of uttering little squeaks of warning.

THEORIST: The new ball!

BOTHAM: Oh, yes?

THEORIST: You don't understand. Lillee and Alderman are taking the new ball.

BOTHAM: Dennis and Terry? Good chaps, I like 'em.

THEORIST: The shine on a new ball dazzles, the seam it cuts!

BOTHAM: Then the best thing is to remove the shine and flatten the seam.

THEORIST: That will take hours.

BOTHAM: Not if the new ball is hit hard enough and often enough. Now shut up and go away because Lillee has bowled me a bouncer and it's about to hit me in the centre of the forehead . . .

This Lillee bouncer did not hit Botham in the centre of the forehead because the batsman hooked it for 6. In the same over Botham repeated the stroke, though on this occasion the crowd at long-leg waved flags (courtesy, presumably, of the Prince and Princess of Wales) and danced. From the new ball Botham scored 90 runs from 49 deliveries – the only quibble being that for some time the ball had ceased, save by the most pedantic definition, to be new. Botham's 118 came in 122 minutes, with six 6s and thirteen 4s.

The wonder of it still dazzles. If we need proof that this was how the cricketers of the Golden Age *tried* to play, let's consult Ranjitsinhji's *Jubilee Book of Cricket* (1897) and glance at the field placings for Tom Richardson, one of the greatest of all fast bowlers. Included is a long-on, a position occupied because batsmen liked to drive Richardson. That few were good enough to do so is neither here nor there; batsmen tried to drive Richardson and, we may surmise, sometimes succeeded because the stroke summed up their attitude towards cricket.

Botham's attitude was summed up at Old Trafford in 1981: 'Well, Dennis, it's either me or you!' To savour the absurdity of that 118 we must note three figures:

1. When Botham came in at 104 for 5, England's batsmen had scored at a rate of 24 runs per 100 balls.

2. Ten England batsmen before, during, and after the Botham interlude scored at a rate of 33 runs per 100 balls.

3. Botham's 118 was scored at a rate of 115 runs per 100 balls.

Cricket is a team game; any one of the deliveries successfully countered by Boycott or Tavaré might have dismissed Botham. But alone of contemporary England cricketers Botham has the skill, the strokes, the power and the belief in himself to raise a match from the ordinary to the fantastic, to those realms of the imagination in which heroes long since dead play at will legendary innings, bowl out the opposition, and make catches impossible for mere mortals. It must be pleasant to be an immortal in one's mid-twenties. Botham's admirers are pleased with his progress thus far; fervently they urge him always to be true to himself.